a Daily Captions five-year journal

Author:

_____

Beginning Date:

_____

Ending Date:

_____

Contact Info:

_____

_____

THESE PAGES ARE YOURS TO FILL.

"Everyone must leave something behind . . . It doesn't matter what you do, so long as you change something from the way it was before you touched it into something that's like you after you take your hands away."

—Ray Bradbury

JANUARY 1

"If I'd observed all the rules, I'd never have got anywhere."

—MARILYN MONROE

20 ___ _____

_____

_____

_____

_____

20 ___ _____

_____

_____

_____

_____

20 ___ _____

_____

_____

_____

_____

20 ___ _____

_____

_____

_____

_____

20 ___ _____

_____

_____

_____

_____

JANUARY 2

"Be yourself; everyone else is already taken."

—OSCAR WILDE

20 ___ _____

_____

_____

_____

20 ___ _____

_____

_____

_____

20 ___ _____

_____

_____

_____

20 ___ _____

_____

_____

_____

20 ___ _____

_____

_____

_____

JANUARY 3

"A friend is someone who knows all about you and still loves you."

— ELBERT HUBBARD

20 ___ _____

_____

_____

_____

20 ___ _____

_____

_____

_____

20 ___ _____

_____

_____

_____

20 ___ _____

_____

_____

_____

20 ___ _____

_____

_____

_____

JANUARY 4

"Be careful about reading health books. You may die of a misprint."

—MARK TWAIN

20 ___ _____

_____

_____

_____

20 ___ _____

_____

_____

_____

20 ___ _____

_____

_____

_____

20 ___ _____

_____

_____

_____

20 ___ _____

_____

_____

_____

JANUARY 5

"Fairy tales are more than true. Not because they tell us that dragons exist, but because they tell us that dragons can be defeated."

— G.K. CHESTERTON

20 ___ _____

_____

_____

_____

20 ___ _____

_____

_____

_____

20 ___ _____

_____

_____

_____

20 ___ _____

_____

_____

_____

20 ___ _____

_____

_____

_____

JANUARY 6

"Reality is merely an illusion, albeit a very persistent one."

—ALBERT EINSTEIN

20 ___ _____

_____

_____

_____

20 ___ _____

_____

_____

_____

20 ___ _____

_____

_____

_____

20 ___ _____

_____

_____

_____

20 ___ _____

_____

_____

_____

JANUARY 7

"To live is the rarest thing in the world. Most people exist, that is all."

—OSCAR WILDE

20 ___ _____

_____

_____

_____

20 ___ _____

_____

_____

_____

20 ___ _____

_____

_____

_____

20 ___ _____

_____

_____

_____

20 ___ _____

_____

_____

_____

JANUARY 8

"It's never too late to be what you might have been."

—GEORGE ELIOT

20 __ _____

_____

_____

_____

_____

20 __ _____

_____

_____

_____

_____

20 __ _____

_____

_____

_____

_____

20 __ _____

_____

_____

_____

_____

20 __ _____

_____

_____

_____

_____

JANUARY 9

"Love all, trust a few, do wrong to none."

—WILLIAM SHAKESPEARE

20 ___ _____

_____

_____

_____

20 ___ _____

_____

_____

_____

20 ___ _____

_____

_____

_____

20 ___ _____

_____

_____

_____

20 ___ _____

_____

_____

_____

JANUARY 10

"I like nonsense; it wakes up the brain cells."

20 __ _____

_____

_____

_____

_____

20 __ _____

_____

_____

_____

_____

20 __ _____

_____

_____

_____

_____

20 __ _____

_____

_____

_____

_____

20 __ _____

_____

_____

_____

_____

JANUARY 11

"I may not have gone where I intended to go, but I think I have ended up where I needed to be."

—DOUGLAS ADAMS

20 ___ _____

_____

_____

_____

20 ___ _____

_____

_____

_____

20 ___ _____

_____

_____

_____

20 ___ _____

_____

_____

_____

20 ___ _____

_____

_____

_____

JANUARY 12

"Be nice to nerds. Chances are you'll end up working for one."

—BILL GATES

20 _____ _____

_____

_____

_____

_____

20 _____ _____

_____

_____

_____

_____

20 _____ _____

_____

_____

_____

_____

20 _____ _____

_____

_____

_____

_____

20 _____ _____

_____

_____

_____

_____

JANUARY 13

"We don't see things as they are; we see them as we are."

—ANAIS NIN

20 ___ _____

_____

_____

_____

_____

20 ___ _____

_____

_____

_____

_____

20 ___ _____

_____

_____

_____

_____

20 ___ _____

_____

_____

_____

_____

20 ___ _____

_____

_____

_____

_____

JANUARY 14

"I have never let my schooling interfere with my education."

—MARK TWAIN

20 __ _____

_____

_____

_____

_____

20 __ _____

_____

_____

_____

_____

20 __ _____

_____

_____

_____

_____

20 __ _____

_____

_____

_____

_____

20 __ _____

_____

_____

_____

_____

JANUARY 15

"The trouble with having an open mind, of course, is that people will insist on coming along and trying to put things in it."

—TERRY PRATCHETT

20 ___ _____

_____

_____

_____

20 ___ _____

_____

_____

_____

20 ___ _____

_____

_____

_____

20 ___ _____

_____

_____

_____

20 ___ _____

_____

_____

_____

JANUARY 16

"If you want to know what a man's like, take a good look at how he treats his inferiors, not his equals."

—J.K. ROWLING

20 ___

_____

_____

_____

_____

20 ___

_____

_____

_____

_____

20 ___

_____

_____

_____

_____

20 ___

_____

_____

_____

_____

20 ___

_____

_____

_____

_____

JANUARY 17

"I have not failed. I've just found 10,000 ways that won't work."

—Thomas A. Edison

20 ___ _____

_____

_____

_____

20 ___ _____

_____

_____

_____

20 ___ _____

_____

_____

_____

20 ___ _____

_____

_____

_____

20 ___ _____

_____

_____

_____

JANUARY 18

"I'm not afraid of death; I just don't want to be there when it happens."

—WOODY ALLEN

20 ___ _____

_____

_____

_____

_____

20 ___ _____

_____

_____

_____

_____

20 ___ _____

_____

_____

_____

_____

20 ___ _____

_____

_____

_____

_____

20 ___ _____

_____

_____

_____

_____

JANUARY 19

"Reality continues to ruin my life."

—BILL WATTERSON

20 ___ _____

_____

_____

_____

20 ___ _____

_____

_____

_____

20 ___ _____

_____

_____

_____

20 ___ _____

_____

_____

_____

20 ___ _____

_____

_____

_____

JANUARY 20

"Darkness cannot drive out darkness; only light can do that. Hate cannot drive out hate; only love can do that."

—MARTIN LUTHER KING, JR.

20 __ _____

_____

_____

_____

20 __ _____

_____

_____

_____

20 __ _____

_____

_____

_____

20 __ _____

_____

_____

_____

20 __ _____

_____

_____

_____

JANUARY 21

"Women are like teabags; you never know how strong they are until they're put in hot water."

—MARILYN MONROE

20 ___ _____

_____

_____

_____

20 ___ _____

_____

_____

_____

20 ___ _____

_____

_____

_____

20 ___ _____

_____

_____

_____

20 ___ _____

_____

_____

_____

JANUARY 22

"Life is what happens to you while you're busy making other plans."

—JOHN LENNON

20 ___ _____

_____

_____

_____

_____

20 ___ _____

_____

_____

_____

_____

20 ___ _____

_____

_____

_____

_____

20 ___ _____

_____

_____

_____

_____

20 ___ _____

_____

_____

_____

_____

JANUARY 23

"I am so clever that sometimes I don't understand a single word of what I am saying."

—MARILYN MONROE

20 ___ _____

_____

_____

_____

20 ___ _____

_____

_____

_____

20 ___ _____

_____

_____

_____

20 ___ _____

_____

_____

_____

20 ___ _____

_____

_____

_____

JANUARY 24

"Live as if you were to die tomorrow. Learn as if you were to live forever."

—MAHATMA GANDHI

20 ___ _____

_____

_____

_____

20 ___ _____

_____

_____

_____

20 ___ _____

_____

_____

_____

20 ___ _____

_____

_____

_____

20 ___ _____

_____

_____

_____

JANUARY 25

"You only live once, but if you do it right, once is enough."

—MAE WEST

20 ___ _____

_____

_____

_____

20 ___ _____

_____

_____

_____

20 ___ _____

_____

_____

_____

20 ___ _____

_____

_____

_____

20 ___ _____

_____

_____

_____

JANUARY 26

"It is very easy to defeat someone,
but it is very hard to win someone."

—Dr. Abdul Kalaam

20 ___

_____

20 ___

_____

20 ___

_____

20 ___

_____

20 ___

_____

JANUARY 27

"It is better to remain silent and be thought a fool than to open one's mouth and remove all doubt."

—ABRAHAM LINCOLN

20 ___ _____

_____

_____

_____

20 ___ _____

_____

_____

_____

_____

20 ___ _____

_____

_____

_____

20 ___ _____

_____

_____

_____

20 ___ _____

_____

_____

_____

JANUARY 28

"Insanity: Doing the same thing over and over again and expecting different results."

—ALBERT EINSTEIN

20 __ _____

_____

_____

_____

20 __ _____

_____

_____

_____

20 __ _____

_____

_____

_____

20 __ _____

_____

_____

_____

20 __ _____

_____

_____

_____

JANUARY 29

"If you tell the truth, you don't have to remember anything."

20 ___ _____

_____

_____

_____

20 ___ _____

_____

_____

_____

20 ___ _____

_____

_____

_____

20 ___ _____

_____

_____

_____

20 ___ _____

_____

_____

_____

JANUARY 30

"The question isn't who is going to let me;
it's who is going to stop me."

20 ___ _____

_____

_____

_____

_____

20 ___ _____

_____

_____

_____

_____

20 ___ _____

_____

_____

_____

_____

20 ___ _____

_____

_____

_____

_____

20 ___ _____

_____

_____

_____

_____

JANUARY 31

"Things are not what they appear to be; nor are they otherwise."

—SURANGAMA SUTRA

20 ___ _____

_____

_____

_____

_____

20 ___ _____

_____

_____

_____

_____

20 ___ _____

_____

_____

_____

_____

20 ___ _____

_____

_____

_____

_____

20 ___ _____

_____

_____

_____

_____

FEBRUARY 1

"Nobody can make you feel inferior without your consent."

—ELEANOR ROOSEVELT

20 ___ _____

_____

_____

_____

_____

20 ___ _____

_____

_____

_____

_____

20 ___ _____

_____

_____

_____

_____

20 ___ _____

_____

_____

_____

_____

20 ___ _____

_____

_____

_____

_____

FEBRUARY 2

"I'm thankful to all those who said NO to me.
Because of them I did it myself."

—ALBERT EINSTEIN

20 ___ _____

_____
_____
_____

20 ___ _____

_____
_____
_____

20 ___ _____

_____
_____
_____

20 ___ _____

_____
_____
_____

20 ___ _____

_____
_____
_____

FEBRUARY 3

"Anyone who lives within their means suffers from a lack of imagination."

—OSCAR WILDE

20 ___ _____

_____

_____

_____

20 ___ _____

_____

_____

_____

20 ___ _____

_____

_____

_____

20 ___ _____

_____

_____

_____

20 ___ _____

_____

_____

_____

FEBRUARY 4

*"Anyone who has never made a mistake
has never tried anything new."*

—ALBERT EINSTEIN

20 __ _____

_____

_____

_____

20 __ _____

_____

_____

_____

20 __ _____

_____

_____

_____

20 __ _____

_____

_____

_____

20 __ _____

_____

_____

_____

FEBRUARY 5

"Today you are You, that is truer than true. There is no one alive who is Youer than You."

20 ___ _____

_____

_____

_____

20 ___ _____

_____

_____

_____

20 ___ _____

_____

_____

_____

20 ___ _____

_____

_____

_____

20 ___ _____

_____

_____

_____

FEBRUARY 6

"You don't have to burn books to destroy a culture. Just get people to stop reading them."

—RAY BRADBURY

20 ___ _____

_____

_____

_____

20 ___ _____

_____

_____

_____

20 ___ _____

_____

_____

_____

20 ___ _____

_____

_____

_____

20 ___ _____

_____

_____

_____

FEBRUARY 7

"How wonderful it is that nobody need wait a single moment before starting to improve the world."

—ANNE FRANK

20 ___ _____

_____

_____

_____

20 ___ _____

_____

_____

_____

20 ___ _____

_____

_____

_____

20 ___ _____

_____

_____

_____

20 ___ _____

_____

_____

_____

FEBRUARY 8

"I know God won't give me anything I can't handle. I just wish he didn't trust me so much."

—MOTHER TERESA

20 ___ _____

_____

_____

_____

20 ___ _____

_____

_____

_____

20 ___ _____

_____

_____

_____

20 ___ _____

_____

_____

_____

20 ___ _____

_____

_____

_____

FEBRUARY 9

"Whether you think you can, or you think you can't--you're right."

—HENRY FORD

20 ___ _____

_____

_____

_____

20 ___ _____

_____

_____

_____

20 ___ _____

_____

_____

_____

20 ___ _____

_____

_____

_____

20 ___ _____

_____

_____

_____

FEBRUARY 10

"Two wrongs don't make a right, but they make a good excuse."

—THOMAS STEPHEN SZASZ

20 ___ _____

_____
_____
_____
_____

20 ___ _____

_____
_____
_____
_____

20 ___ _____

_____
_____
_____
_____

20 ___ _____

_____
_____
_____
_____

20 ___ _____

_____
_____
_____
_____

FEBRUARY 11

*"The fear of death follows from the fear of life. A man who lives
fully is prepared to die at any time."*

20 ___ _____

_____

_____

_____

20 ___ _____

_____

_____

_____

20 ___ _____

_____

_____

_____

20 ___ _____

_____

_____

_____

20 ___ _____

_____

_____

_____

FEBRUARY 12

"If we knew what we were doing, it would not be called research, would it?"

—ALBERT EINSTEIN

20 ___ _____

_____

_____

_____

20 ___ _____

_____

_____

_____

20 ___ _____

_____

_____

_____

20 ___ _____

_____

_____

_____

20 ___ _____

_____

_____

_____

FEBRUARY 13

"The Guide says there is an art to flying…or rather a knack. The knack lies in learning to throw yourself at the ground and miss."
—Douglas Adams

20 ___ _____

_____

_____

_____

_____

20 ___ _____

_____

_____

_____

_____

20 ___ _____

_____

_____

_____

_____

20 ___ _____

_____

_____

_____

_____

20 ___ _____

_____

_____

_____

_____

FEBRUARY 14

"You know you're in love when you can't fall asleep because reality is finally better than your dreams."

20 ___ _____

_____

_____

_____

20 ___ _____

_____

_____

_____

20 ___ _____

_____

_____

_____

20 ___ _____

_____

_____

_____

20 ___ _____

_____

_____

_____

FEBRUARY 15

"The cure for boredom is curiosity. There is no cure for curiosity."

—DOROTHY PARKER

20 ___ _____

_____

_____

_____

_____

20 ___ _____

_____

_____

_____

_____

20 ___ _____

_____

_____

_____

20 ___ _____

_____

_____

_____

20 ___ _____

_____

_____

_____

FEBRUARY 16

"Choose a job you love, and you will never have to work a day in your life."

—MARILYN MONROE

20 ___ _____

_____

_____

_____

20 ___ _____

_____

_____

_____

20 ___ _____

_____

_____

_____

20 ___ _____

_____

_____

_____

20 ___ _____

_____

_____

_____

FEBRUARY 17

"What lies behind us and what lies before us are tiny matters compared to what lies within us."

—RALPH WALDO EMERSON

20 17 Struggling today. Big fight last night
w/Ben about church. Feels like I have no safe
place to turn.
Psalm 25:16

20 __

20 __

20 __

20 __

FEBRUARY 18

"Reader, suppose you were an idiot. And suppose you were a member of Congress. But I repeat myself."

—MARK TWAIN

20 __ _____

_____

_____

_____

20 __ _____

_____

_____

_____

20 __ _____

_____

_____

_____

20 __ _____

_____

_____

_____

20 __ _____

_____

_____

_____

FEBRUARY 19

"To love would be an awfully big adventure."

20 __ _____

_____

_____

_____

20 __ _____

_____

_____

_____

20 __ _____

_____

_____

_____

20 __ _____

_____

_____

_____

20 __ _____

_____

_____

_____

FEBRUARY 20

"I think she's having hysterics. Maybe you should slap her."

20 ___ _____

_____
_____
_____
_____

20 ___ _____

_____
_____
_____
_____

20 ___ _____

_____
_____
_____
_____

20 ___ _____

_____
_____
_____
_____

20 ___ _____

_____
_____
_____
_____

FEBRUARY 21

"It does not do to dwell on dreams and forget to live."

—J.K. ROWLING

20 __ _____

_____

_____

_____

_____

20 __ _____

_____

_____

_____

_____

20 __ _____

_____

_____

_____

_____

20 __ _____

_____

_____

_____

_____

20 __ _____

_____

_____

_____

_____

FEBRUARY 22

"Creativity is knowing how to hide your sources."

—ALBERT EINSTEIN

20 __ _____

20 __ _____

20 __ _____

20 __ _____

20 __ _____

FEBRUARY 23

*"The really great people make you feel that you, too,
can become great."*

—MARK TWAIN

20 ___ _____

_____

_____

_____

_____

20 ___ _____

_____

_____

_____

_____

20 ___ _____

_____

_____

_____

_____

20 ___ _____

_____

_____

_____

_____

20 ___ _____

_____

_____

_____

_____

FEBRUARY 24

"If friendship is your weakest point, then you are the strongest person in the world."

—ABRAHAM LINCOLN

20 ___ _____

_____

_____

_____

20 ___ _____

_____

_____

_____

20 ___ _____

_____

_____

_____

20 ___ _____

_____

_____

_____

20 ___ _____

_____

_____

_____

FEBRUARY 25

"Go to heaven for the climate and hell for the company."

—MARK TWAIN

20 ___ _____

_____

_____

_____

20 ___ _____

_____

_____

_____

20 ___ _____

_____

_____

_____

20 ___ _____

_____

_____

_____

20 ___ _____

_____

_____

_____

FEBRUARY 26

"Everything you can imagine is real."

—PABLO PICASSO

20 ___ _____

_____

_____

_____

20 ___ _____

_____

_____

_____

20 ___ _____

_____

_____

_____

20 ___ _____

_____

_____

_____

20 ___ _____

_____

_____

_____

FEBRUARY 27

"You may say I'm a dreamer, but I'm not the only one. I hope someday you'll join us. And the world will live as one."

—JOHN LENNON

20 __ _____

_____

_____

_____

20 __ _____

_____

_____

_____

20 __ _____

_____

_____

_____

20 __ _____

_____

_____

_____

20 __ _____

_____

_____

_____

FEBRUARY 28

"Success is not final, failure is not fatal: it is the courage to continue that counts."

—WINSTON CHURCHILL

20 ___

20 ___

20 ___

20 ___

20 ___

FEBRUARY 29 (LEAP YEAR)

"May the odds be ever in your favor."

—SUZANNE COLLINS

20 __ _____

_____

_____

_____

20 __ _____

_____

_____

_____

20 __ _____

_____

_____

_____

20 __ _____

_____

_____

_____

20 __ _____

_____

_____

_____

MARCH 1

"We become what we think about."

—EARL NIGHTINGALE

20 ___ _____

_____

_____

_____

20 ___ _____

_____

_____

_____

20 ___ _____

_____

_____

_____

20 ___ _____

_____

_____

_____

20 ___ _____

_____

_____

_____

MARCH 2

*"A pessimist sees the difficulty in every opportunity; an optimist
sees the opportunity in every difficulty."*

—WINSTON CHURCHILL

20 ___ _____

_____

_____

_____

20 ___ _____

_____

_____

_____

20 ___ _____

_____

_____

_____

20 ___ _____

_____

_____

_____

20 ___ _____

_____

_____

_____

MARCH 3

"Don't wait. The time will never be just right."

—NAPOLEON HILL

20 ___

_____

_____

_____

_____

20 ___

_____

_____

_____

_____

20 ___

_____

_____

_____

20 ___

_____

_____

_____

_____

20 ___

_____

_____

_____

_____

MARCH 4

"Either you run the day, or the day runs you."

—JIM ROHN

20 ___ _____

_____

_____

_____

20 ___ _____

_____

_____

_____

20 ___ _____

_____

_____

_____

20 ___ _____

_____

_____

_____

20 ___ _____

_____

_____

_____

MARCH 5

"A day without sunshine is like, you know, night."

—STEVE MARTIN

20 ___ _____

_____
_____
_____
_____

20 ___ _____

_____
_____
_____
_____

20 ___ _____

_____
_____
_____
_____

20 ___ _____

_____
_____
_____
_____

20 ___ _____

_____
_____
_____
_____

MARCH 6

"That which does not kill us makes us stronger."

— FRIEDRICH WILHELM NIETZSCHE

20 _____ _____

_____

_____

_____

_____

20 _____ _____

_____

_____

_____

_____

20 _____ _____

_____

_____

_____

_____

20 _____ _____

_____

_____

_____

_____

20 _____ _____

_____

_____

_____

_____

MARCH 7

"When I let go of what I am, I become what I might be."

—LAO TZU

20 ___ _____

_____

_____

_____

20 ___ _____

_____

_____

_____

20 ___ _____

_____

_____

_____

20 ___ _____

_____

_____

_____

20 ___ _____

_____

_____

_____

MARCH 8

"Always forgive your enemies; nothing annoys them so much."

20 ___ _____

_____

_____

_____

_____

20 ___ _____

_____

_____

_____

_____

20 ___ _____

_____

_____

_____

_____

20 ___ _____

_____

_____

_____

_____

20 ___ _____

_____

_____

_____

_____

MARCH 9

"Yesterday is history. Tomorrow is a mystery. Today is a gift. That's why we call it 'The Present'."

—ELEANOR ROOSEVELT

20 ___ _____

_____

_____

_____

_____

20 ___ _____

_____

_____

_____

_____

20 ___ _____

_____

_____

_____

_____

20 ___ _____

_____

_____

_____

_____

20 ___ _____

_____

_____

_____

_____

MARCH 10

"In the beginning the Universe was created. This has made a lot of people very angry and been widely regarded as a bad move."

—DOUGLAS ADAMS

20 ___ _____

_____

_____

_____

_____

20 ___ _____

_____

_____

_____

_____

20 ___ _____

_____

_____

_____

_____

20 ___ _____

_____

_____

_____

_____

20 ___ _____

_____

_____

_____

_____

MARCH 11

"Whenever you find yourself on the side of the majority, it is time to pause and reflect."

—MARK TWAIN

20 ___ _____

_____

_____

_____

20 ___ _____

_____

_____

_____

20 ___ _____

_____

_____

_____

20 ___ _____

_____

_____

_____

20 ___ _____

_____

_____

_____

MARCH 12

"It's not true that I had nothing on. I had the radio on."

—MARILYN MONROE

20 ___ _____

_____

_____

_____

_____

20 ___ _____

_____

_____

_____

_____

20 ___ _____

_____

_____

_____

_____

20 ___ _____

_____

_____

_____

_____

20 ___ _____

_____

_____

_____

_____

MARCH 13

"If you don't stand for something you will fall for anything."

—MALCOLM X

20 ___ _____

_____

_____

_____

_____

20 ___ _____

_____

_____

_____

_____

20 ___ _____

_____

_____

_____

_____

20 ___ _____

_____

_____

_____

_____

20 ___ _____

_____

_____

_____

_____

MARCH 14

"In three words I can sum up everything I've learned about life: it goes on."

—ROBERT FROST

20 ___ _____

_____

_____

_____

20 ___ _____

_____

_____

_____

20 ___ _____

_____

_____

_____

20 ___ _____

_____

_____

_____

20 ___ _____

_____

_____

_____

MARCH 15

"To be yourself in a world that is constantly trying to make you something else is the greatest accomplishment."

—RALPH WALDO EMERSON

20 ___ _____

_____

_____

_____

20 ___ _____

_____

_____

_____

20 ___ _____

_____

_____

_____

20 ___ _____

_____

_____

_____

20 ___ _____

_____

_____

_____

MARCH 16

"Imagination is more important than knowledge. Knowledge is limited. Imagination encircles the world."

—ALBERT EINSTEIN

20 ___ _____

_____

_____

_____

_____

20 ___ _____

_____

_____

_____

_____

20 ___ _____

_____

_____

_____

_____

20 ___ _____

_____

_____

_____

_____

20 ___ _____

_____

_____

_____

_____

MARCH 17

"Science without religion is lame, religion without science is blind."

—ALBERT EINSTEIN

20 ___ _____

_____

_____

_____

_____

20 ___ _____

_____

_____

_____

_____

20 ___ _____

_____

_____

_____

_____

20 ___ _____

_____

_____

_____

_____

20 ___ _____

_____

_____

_____

_____

MARCH 18

"People will forget what you said, people will forget what you did, but people will never forget how you made them feel."

—MAYA ANGELOU

20 ___

_____

_____

_____

_____

20 ___

_____

_____

_____

_____

20 ___

_____

_____

_____

_____

20 ___

_____

_____

_____

_____

20 ___

_____

_____

_____

_____

MARCH 19

"Women and cats will do as they please, and men and dogs should relax and get used to the idea."

20 ___ _____

_____

_____

_____

20 ___ _____

_____

_____

_____

20 ___ _____

_____

_____

_____

20 ___ _____

_____

_____

_____

20 ___ _____

_____

_____

_____

MARCH 20

"All you need is love. But a little chocolate now and then doesn't hurt."

—Charles M. Schulz

20 ___ _____

_____

_____

_____

20 ___ _____

_____

_____

_____

20 ___ _____

_____

_____

_____

20 ___ _____

_____

_____

_____

20 ___ _____

_____

_____

_____

MARCH 21

"It is better to be hated for what you are than loved for what you are not."

—ANDRE GIDE

20 _____ _____

_____

_____

_____

20 _____ _____

_____

_____

_____

20 _____ _____

_____

_____

_____

20 _____ _____

_____

_____

_____

20 _____ _____

_____

_____

_____

MARCH 22

"Peace begins with a smile."

—MOTHER TERESA

20 ___ _____

_____

_____

_____

_____

20 ___ _____

_____

_____

_____

_____

20 ___ _____

_____

_____

_____

_____

20 ___ _____

_____

_____

_____

_____

20 ___ _____

_____

_____

_____

_____

MARCH 23

"Success is often achieved by those who don't know that failure is inevitable."

—COCO CHANEL

20 ___ _____

_____

_____

_____

20 ___ _____

_____

_____

_____

20 ___ _____

_____

_____

_____

20 ___ _____

_____

_____

_____

20 ___ _____

_____

_____

_____

MARCH 24

"What people are ashamed of usually makes a good story."

—F. SCOTT FITZGERALD

20 ___ _____

_____

_____

_____

20 ___ _____

_____

_____

_____

20 ___ _____

_____

_____

_____

20 ___ _____

_____

_____

_____

20 ___ _____

_____

_____

_____

MARCH 25

"We must not allow the clock and the calendar to blind us to the fact that each moment of life is a miracle and mystery."

—H.G. WELLS

20 ___

_____

_____

_____

_____

20 ___

_____

_____

_____

_____

20 ___

_____

_____

_____

_____

20 ___

_____

_____

_____

_____

20 ___

_____

_____

_____

_____

MARCH 26

*"Be still when you have nothing to say; when genuine passion
moves you, say what you've got to say, and say it hot."*

—D.H. LAWRENCE

20 __ _____

_____

_____

_____

_____

20 __ _____

_____

_____

_____

_____

20 __ _____

_____

_____

_____

_____

20 __ _____

_____

_____

_____

_____

20 __ _____

_____

_____

_____

_____

MARCH 27

"Facts do not cease to exist because they are ignored."

—ALDOUS HUXLEY

20 ___ _____

_____

_____

_____

20 ___ _____

_____

_____

_____

20 ___ _____

_____

_____

_____

20 ___ _____

_____

_____

_____

20 ___ _____

_____

_____

_____

MARCH 28

"Without deviation from the norm, progress is not possible."

—FRANK ZAPPA

20 __ _____

_____

_____

_____

20 __ _____

_____

_____

_____

20 __ _____

_____

_____

_____

20 __ _____

_____

_____

_____

20 __ _____

_____

_____

_____

MARCH 29

"The difference between genius and stupidity is; genius has its limits."

—ALBERT EINSTEIN

20 ___ _____

_____

_____

_____

20 ___ _____

_____

_____

_____

20 ___ _____

_____

_____

_____

20 ___ _____

_____

_____

_____

20 ___ _____

_____

_____

_____

MARCH 30

"Dreaming, after all, is a form of planning."

—GLORIA STEINEM

20 ___ _____

_____

_____

_____

_____

20 ___ _____

_____

_____

_____

_____

20 ___ _____

_____

_____

_____

_____

20 ___ _____

_____

_____

_____

_____

20 ___ _____

_____

_____

_____

_____

MARCH 31

"Faith is taking the first step even when you can't see the whole staircase."

— MARTIN LUTHER KING JR.

20 ___ _____

_____

_____

_____

20 ___ _____

_____

_____

_____

20 ___ _____

_____

_____

_____

20 ___ _____

_____

_____

_____

20 ___ _____

_____

_____

_____

APRIL 1

"When people are free to do as they please,
they usually imitate each other."

—ERIC HOFFER

20 ___ _____

_____

_____

_____

20 ___ _____

_____

_____

_____

20 ___ _____

_____

_____

_____

20 ___ _____

_____

_____

_____

20 ___ _____

_____

_____

_____

APRIL 2

"Time you enjoy wasting, was not wasted."

—JOHN LENNON

20 ___

20 ___

20 ___

20 ___

20 ___

APRIL 3

"It's the friends you can call up at 4 a.m. that matter."

—MARLENE DIETRICH

20 ___ _____

_____

_____

_____

20 ___ _____

_____

_____

_____

20 ___ _____

_____

_____

_____

20 ___ _____

_____

_____

_____

20 ___ _____

_____

_____

_____

APRIL 4

"Oh, what a tangled web do parents weave, when they think that their children are naive."

—OGDEN NASH

20 ___

20 ___

20 ___

20 ___

20 ___

APRIL 5

"It's better to be looked over than overlooked."

—MAE WEST

20 ___

_____

_____

_____

_____

_____

20 ___

_____

_____

_____

_____

_____

20 ___

_____

_____

_____

_____

_____

20 ___

_____

_____

_____

_____

_____

20 ___

_____

_____

_____

_____

_____

APRIL 6

"Immature poets imitate; mature poets steal."

–T.S. Eliot

20 __ _____

_____

_____

_____

20 __ _____

_____

_____

_____

20 __ _____

_____

_____

_____

20 __ _____

_____

_____

_____

20 __ _____

_____

_____

_____

APRIL 7

"Dreams at first seem impossible, then they seem improbable, and then when we summon the will, they soon become inevitable."
—CHRISTOPHER REEVE

20 ___ _____

_____

_____

_____

_____

20 ___ _____

_____

_____

_____

_____

20 ___ _____

_____

_____

_____

_____

20 ___ _____

_____

_____

_____

_____

20 ___ _____

_____

_____

_____

_____

APRIL 8

"If there is no struggle, there is no progress."

—FREDERICK DOUGLAS

20 ___

_____

20 ___

_____

20 ___

_____

20 ___

_____

20 ___

_____

APRIL 9

"A little nonsense now and then, is cherished by the wisest men."

—ROALD DAHL

20 ___ _____

_____

_____

_____

_____

20 ___ _____

_____

_____

_____

_____

20 ___ _____

_____

_____

_____

_____

20 ___ _____

_____

_____

_____

_____

20 ___ _____

_____

_____

_____

_____

APRIL 10

"It does not require a majority to prevail, but rather an irate, tireless minority keen to set brush fires in people's minds."

—SAMUEL ADAMS

20 __ _____

_____

_____

_____

20 __ _____

_____

_____

_____

20 __ _____

_____

_____

_____

20 __ _____

_____

_____

_____

20 __ _____

_____

_____

_____

APRIL 11

"You cannot find peace by avoiding life."

—VIRGINIA WOOLF

20 ___ _____

_____

_____

_____

_____

20 ___ _____

_____

_____

_____

_____

20 ___ _____

_____

_____

_____

_____

20 ___ _____

_____

_____

_____

_____

20 ___ _____

_____

_____

_____

_____

APRIL 12

"Truth is stranger than fiction, but it is because Fiction is obliged to stick to possibilities; Truth isn't."

—MARK TWAIN

20 ___ _____

_____

_____

_____

20 ___ _____

_____

_____

_____

20 ___ _____

_____

_____

_____

20 ___ _____

_____

_____

_____

20 ___ _____

_____

_____

_____

APRIL 13

"First they ignore you, then they ridicule you, then they fight you, and then you win."

—Mahatma Gandhi

20 ___ _____

_____

_____

_____

_____

20 ___ _____

_____

_____

_____

_____

20 ___ _____

_____

_____

_____

_____

20 ___ _____

_____

_____

_____

_____

20 ___ _____

_____

_____

_____

_____

APRIL 14

"Of all sad words of tongue or pen, the saddest are these,
'It might have been.'"

—JOHN GREENLEAF WHITTIER

20 _____ _____

_____

_____

_____

_____

20 _____ _____

_____

_____

_____

_____

20 _____ _____

_____

_____

_____

_____

20 _____ _____

_____

_____

_____

_____

20 _____ _____

_____

_____

_____

_____

APRIL 15

"It is better to keep your mouth closed and let people think you are a fool than to open it and remove all doubt."

—MARK TWAIN

20 ___ _____

_____

_____

_____

_____

20 ___ _____

_____

_____

_____

_____

20 ___ _____

_____

_____

_____

_____

20 ___ _____

_____

_____

_____

_____

20 ___ _____

_____

_____

_____

_____

APRIL 16

"If you want your children to be intelligent, read them fairy tales. If you want them to be more intelligent, read them more fairy tales."
—ALBERT EINSTEIN

20 ___ _____

_____

_____

_____

20 ___ _____

_____

_____

_____

20 ___ _____

_____

_____

_____

20 ___ _____

_____

_____

_____

20 ___ _____

_____

_____

_____

APRIL 17

"Life is to be enjoyed, not endured."

—GORDON B. HINCKLEY

20 __ _____

_____

_____

_____

20 __ _____

_____

_____

_____

20 __ _____

_____

_____

_____

20 __ _____

_____

_____

_____

20 __ _____

_____

_____

_____

APRIL 18

"Happiness is when what you think, what you say, and what you do are in harmony."

—MAHATMA GANDHI

20 ___ _____

_____

_____

_____

_____

20 ___ _____

_____

_____

_____

_____

20 ___ _____

_____

_____

_____

_____

20 ___ _____

_____

_____

_____

_____

20 ___ _____

_____

_____

_____

_____

APRIL 19

"I don't know the key to success, but the key to failure is trying to please everyone."

—BILL COSBY

20 ___ _____

_____

_____

_____

_____

20 ___ _____

_____

_____

_____

_____

20 ___ _____

_____

_____

_____

_____

20 ___ _____

_____

_____

_____

_____

20 ___ _____

_____

_____

_____

_____

APRIL 20

"The more that you read, the more things you will know. The more that you learn, the more places you'll go."

—DR. SEUSS

20 ___ _____

_____

_____

_____

20 ___ _____

_____

_____

_____

20 ___ _____

_____

_____

_____

20 ___ _____

_____

_____

_____

20 ___ _____

_____

_____

_____

APRIL 21

"Well-behaved women rarely make history."

—LAUREL THATCHER ULRICH

20 ___ _____

_____

_____

_____

_____

20 ___ _____

_____

_____

_____

_____

20 ___ _____

_____

_____

_____

_____

20 ___ _____

_____

_____

_____

_____

20 ___ _____

_____

_____

_____

_____

APRIL 22

"It takes courage to grow up and become who you really are."

—EE CUMMINGS

20 ___

_____

_____

_____

_____

20 ___

_____

_____

_____

_____

20 ___

_____

_____

_____

_____

20 ___

_____

_____

_____

_____

20 ___

_____

_____

_____

_____

APRIL 23

"The man who does not read good books has no advantage over the man who can't read them."

—MARK TWAIN

20 ___ _____
_____
_____
_____

20 ___ _____
_____
_____
_____

20 ___ _____
_____
_____
_____

20 ___ _____
_____
_____
_____

20 ___ _____
_____
_____
_____

APRIL 24

"Friendship is born at that moment when one person says to another: 'What! You too? I thought I was the only one.'"

—C.S. Lewis

20 ___ _____

_____

_____

_____

20 ___ _____

_____

_____

_____

20 ___ _____

_____

_____

_____

20 ___ _____

_____

_____

_____

20 ___ _____

_____

_____

_____

APRIL 25

"Twenty years from now you will be more disappointed by the things that you didn't do than by the ones you did do."

—MARK TWAIN

20 __ _____

_____

_____

_____

20 __ _____

_____

_____

_____

20 __ _____

_____

_____

_____

20 __ _____

_____

_____

_____

20 __ _____

_____

_____

_____

APRIL 26

*"Soon we must all face the choice between what is right
and what is easy."*

–J.K. ROWLING

20 ___ _____

_____

_____

_____

20 ___ _____

_____

_____

_____

20 ___ _____

_____

_____

_____

20 ___ _____

_____

_____

_____

20 ___ _____

_____

_____

_____

APRIL 27

"The willingness to accept responsibility for one's own life is the source from which self-respect springs."

—MARILYN MONROE

20 ___ _____

_____

_____

_____

_____

20 ___ _____

_____

_____

_____

_____

20 ___ _____

_____

_____

_____

_____

20 ___ _____

_____

_____

_____

_____

20 ___ _____

_____

_____

_____

_____

APRIL 28

"Instead of developing your personality, charm or intellect, try exercising your character today."

— STEPHANIE GODDARD DAVIDSON

20 __

_____

20 __

_____

20 __

_____

20 __

_____

20 __

_____

APRIL 29

"They are able because they think they are able."

—VIRGIL

20 ___ _____

_____

_____

_____

20 ___ _____

_____

_____

_____

20 ___ _____

_____

_____

_____

20 ___ _____

_____

_____

_____

20 ___ _____

_____

_____

_____

APRIL 30

"I don't have to be what you want me to be."

—Muhammad Ali

20 ___ _____

_____

_____

_____

20 ___ _____

_____

_____

_____

20 ___ _____

_____

_____

_____

20 ___ _____

_____

_____

_____

20 ___ _____

_____

_____

_____

MAY 1

"Most people are other people. Their thoughts are someone else's opinions, their lives a mimicry, their passions a quotation."

—MARILYN MONROE

20 __ _____

_____

_____

_____

_____

20 __ _____

_____

_____

_____

_____

20 __ _____

_____

_____

_____

_____

20 __ _____

_____

_____

_____

_____

20 __ _____

_____

_____

_____

_____

MAY 2

"There are worse crimes than burning books. One of them is not reading them."

—JOSEPH BRODSKY

20 ___

_____

_____

_____

_____

_____

20 ___

_____

_____

_____

_____

_____

20 ___

_____

_____

_____

_____

20 ___

_____

_____

_____

_____

20 ___

_____

_____

_____

_____

MAY 3

"If you don't stick to your values when they're being tested, they're not values. They're hobbies."

—JOHN STEWART

20 ___ _____

_____

_____

_____

_____

20 ___ _____

_____

_____

_____

_____

20 ___ _____

_____

_____

_____

_____

20 ___ _____

_____

_____

_____

_____

20 ___ _____

_____

_____

_____

_____

MAY 4

"There is only one success: to be able to spend your life in your own way."

—CHRISTOPHER MORLEY

20 ___ _____

_____

_____

_____

_____

20 ___ _____

_____

_____

_____

_____

20 ___ _____

_____

_____

_____

_____

20 ___ _____

_____

_____

_____

_____

20 ___ _____

_____

_____

_____

_____

MAY 5

"The choice is ours, in every moment."

—M.J. RYAN

20 ___ _____

_____

_____

_____

_____

20 ___ _____

_____

_____

_____

_____

20 ___ _____

_____

_____

_____

_____

20 ___ _____

_____

_____

_____

_____

20 ___ _____

_____

_____

_____

_____

MAY 6

"I base most of my fashion taste on what doesn't itch."

—GILDA RADNER

20 ___ _____

_____

_____

_____

_____

20 ___ _____

_____

_____

_____

_____

20 ___ _____

_____

_____

_____

_____

20 ___ _____

_____

_____

_____

_____

20 ___ _____

_____

_____

_____

_____

MAY 7

"Your future depends on many things, but mostly on you."

—FRANK TYGER

20 ___ _____

_____

_____

_____

_____

20 ___ _____

_____

_____

_____

_____

20 ___ _____

_____

_____

_____

_____

20 ___ _____

_____

_____

_____

_____

20 ___ _____

_____

_____

_____

_____

MAY 8

"When you least expect it, someone may actually listen to what you have to say."

—MAGGIE KUHN

20 ___

_____

_____

_____

_____

20 ___

_____

_____

_____

_____

20 ___

_____

_____

_____

_____

20 ___

_____

_____

_____

_____

20 ___

_____

_____

_____

_____

MAY 9

"Life loves to be taken by the lapel and told: 'I'm with you kid. Let's go.'"

—MAYA ANGELOU

20 ___ _____

_____

_____

_____

_____

20 ___ _____

_____

_____

_____

_____

20 ___ _____

_____

_____

_____

_____

20 ___ _____

_____

_____

_____

_____

20 ___ _____

_____

_____

_____

_____

MAY 10

"History, despite its wrenching pain, cannot be unlived; but if faced with courage, need not be lived again."

—MAYA ANGELOU

20 ___ _____

_____

_____

_____

20 ___ _____

_____

_____

_____

20 ___ _____

_____

_____

_____

20 ___ _____

_____

_____

_____

20 ___ _____

_____

_____

_____

MAY 11

"I don't want to get to the end of my life and find that I lived just the length of it. I want to have lived the width of it as well."

—DIANE ACKERMAN

20 __ _____

_____

_____

_____

20 __ _____

_____

_____

_____

20 __ _____

_____

_____

_____

20 __ _____

_____

_____

_____

20 __ _____

_____

_____

_____

MAY 12

"Write what should not be forgotten."

— ISABEL ALLENDE

20 ___ _____

_____

_____

_____

20 ___ _____

_____

_____

_____

20 ___ _____

_____

_____

_____

20 ___ _____

_____

_____

_____

20 ___ _____

_____

_____

_____

MAY 13

"You're never too old to become younger."

—Mae West

20 ___ _____

_____

_____

_____

_____

20 ___ _____

_____

_____

_____

_____

20 ___ _____

_____

_____

_____

_____

20 ___ _____

_____

_____

_____

_____

20 ___ _____

_____

_____

_____

_____

MAY 14

"A bird doesn't sing because it has an answer, it sings because it has a song."

—MAYA ANGELOU

20 ___ _____

_____

_____

_____

20 ___ _____

_____

_____

_____

20 ___ _____

_____

_____

_____

20 ___ _____

_____

_____

_____

20 ___ _____

_____

_____

_____

MAY 15

"Talent hits a target no one else can hit; Genius hits a target no one else can see."

—ARTHUR SHOPENHAUER

20 ___ _____

_____

_____

_____

_____

20 ___ _____

_____

_____

_____

_____

20 ___ _____

_____

_____

_____

_____

20 ___ _____

_____

_____

_____

_____

20 ___ _____

_____

_____

_____

_____

MAY 16

"Our lives begin to end the day we become silent about things that matter."

—MARTIN LUTHER KING, JR.

20 ___ _____

_____

_____

_____

20 ___ _____

_____

_____

_____

20 ___ _____

_____

_____

_____

20 ___ _____

_____

_____

_____

20 ___ _____

_____

_____

_____

MAY 17

"Everyone you will ever meet knows something you don't."

—BILL NYE

20 ___ _____

_____

_____

_____

_____

20 ___ _____

_____

_____

_____

_____

20 ___ _____

_____

_____

_____

_____

20 ___ _____

_____

_____

_____

_____

20 ___ _____

_____

_____

_____

_____

MAY 18

"Whatever you are, be a good one."

—ABRAHAM LINCOLN

20 ___ _____

_____

_____

_____

20 ___ _____

_____

_____

_____

20 ___ _____

_____

_____

_____

20 ___ _____

_____

_____

_____

20 ___ _____

_____

_____

_____

MAY 19

"Get busy living or get busy dying."

—STEPHEN KING

20 ___ _____

_____

_____

_____

20 ___ _____

_____

_____

_____

20 ___ _____

_____

_____

_____

20 ___ _____

_____

_____

_____

20 ___ _____

_____

_____

_____

MAY 20

"It is not in the stars to hold our destiny but in ourselves."

—WILLIAM SHAKESPEARE

20 __ _____

_____

_____

_____

20 __ _____

_____

_____

_____

20 __ _____

_____

_____

_____

20 __ _____

_____

_____

_____

20 __ _____

_____

_____

_____

MAY 21

"Coincidence is God's way of remaining anonymous."

—ALBERT EINSTEIN

20 ___ _____

_____

_____

_____

_____

20 ___ _____

_____

_____

_____

_____

20 ___ _____

_____

_____

_____

_____

20 ___ _____

_____

_____

_____

_____

20 ___ _____

_____

_____

_____

_____

MAY 22

"Minds are like parachutes; they only function when they are open."

—SIR JAMES DEWAR

20 ___ _____

_____

_____

_____

20 ___ _____

_____

_____

_____

20 ___ _____

_____

_____

_____

20 ___ _____

_____

_____

_____

20 ___ _____

_____

_____

_____

MAY 23

"Millions long for immortality who do not know what to do with themselves on a rainy Sunday afternoon."

—SUSAN ERTZ

20 ___ _____

_____

_____

_____

20 ___ _____

_____

_____

_____

20 ___ _____

_____

_____

_____

20 ___ _____

_____

_____

_____

20 ___ _____

_____

_____

_____

MAY 24

"Imagination rules the world."

—Napoleon

20 ___ _____

_____

_____

_____

20 ___ _____

_____

_____

_____

20 ___ _____

_____

_____

_____

20 ___ _____

_____

_____

_____

20 ___ _____

_____

_____

_____

MAY 25

"I'm no model lady. A model's just an imitation of the real thing."

—MAE WEST

20 ___ _____

_____

_____

_____

20 ___ _____

_____

_____

_____

20 ___ _____

_____

_____

_____

20 ___ _____

_____

_____

_____

20 ___ _____

_____

_____

_____

MAY 26

"The reason I talk to myself is because I'm the only one whose answers I accept."

—GEORGE CARLIN

20 ___ _____

_____

_____

_____

20 ___ _____

_____

_____

_____

20 ___ _____

_____

_____

_____

20 ___ _____

_____

_____

_____

20 ___ _____

_____

_____

_____

MAY 27

"I like work: it fascinates me. I can sit and look at it for hours."

—JEROME K. JEROME

20 ___ _____

_____

_____

_____

_____

20 ___ _____

_____

_____

_____

_____

20 ___ _____

_____

_____

_____

_____

20 ___ _____

_____

_____

_____

_____

20 ___ _____

_____

_____

_____

_____

MAY 28

"It takes a great deal of bravery to stand up to our enemies, but just as much to stand up to our friends."

–J.K. ROWLING

20 ___ _____

_____

_____

_____

_____

20 ___ _____

_____

_____

_____

_____

20 ___ _____

_____

_____

_____

_____

20 ___ _____

_____

_____

_____

_____

20 ___ _____

_____

_____

_____

_____

MAY 29

"You only live once, but if you do it right, once is enough."

—MAE WEST

20 ___

_____

_____

_____

_____

20 ___

_____

_____

_____

_____

20 ___

_____

_____

_____

_____

20 ___

_____

_____

_____

_____

20 ___

_____

_____

_____

_____

MAY 30

"If you don't know where you are going,
any road will get you there."

—LEWIS CARROL

20 ___ _____

_____

_____

_____

20 ___ _____

_____

_____

_____

20 ___ _____

_____

_____

_____

20 ___ _____

_____

_____

_____

20 ___ _____

_____

_____

_____

MAY 31

"If you can't explain it to a six year old,
you don't understand it yourself."

—ALBERT EINSTEIN

20 __ _____

_____

_____

_____

20 __ _____

_____

_____

_____

20 __ _____

_____

_____

_____

20 __ _____

_____

_____

_____

20 __ _____

_____

_____

_____

JUNE 1

"Whenever I'm caught between two evils,
I take the one I've never tried."

—MAE WEST

20 ___ _____

_____

_____

_____

_____

20 ___ _____

_____

_____

_____

_____

20 ___ _____

_____

_____

_____

_____

20 ___ _____

_____

_____

_____

_____

20 ___ _____

_____

_____

_____

_____

JUNE 2

"There is nothing more uncommon than common sense."

—FRANK LLOYD WRIGHT

20 ___ _____

_____

_____

_____

20 ___ _____

_____

_____

_____

20 ___ _____

_____

_____

_____

20 ___ _____

_____

_____

_____

20 ___ _____

_____

_____

_____

JUNE 3

"It's kind of fun to do the impossible."

—WALT DISNEY

20 ___ _____

_____

_____

_____

20 ___ _____

_____

_____

_____

20 ___ _____

_____

_____

_____

20 ___ _____

_____

_____

_____

20 ___ _____

_____

_____

_____

JUNE 4

"I hate quotations. Tell me what you know."

—RALPH WALDO EMERSON

20 ___

20 ___

20 ___

20 ___

20 ___

JUNE 5

"A dame that knows the ropes isn't likely to get tied up."

—MAE WEST

20 _____ _____

_____

_____

_____

_____

20 _____ _____

_____

_____

_____

_____

20 _____ _____

_____

_____

_____

_____

20 _____ _____

_____

_____

_____

_____

20 _____ _____

_____

_____

_____

_____

JUNE 6

"Don't go around saying the world owes you a living; the world owes you nothing; it was here first."

—MARK TWAIN

20 ___ _____

_____

_____

_____

_____

20 ___ _____

_____

_____

_____

_____

20 ___ _____

_____

_____

_____

_____

20 ___ _____

_____

_____

_____

_____

20 ___ _____

_____

_____

_____

_____

JUNE 7

"Death cannot stop true love. All it can do is delay it for a while."

—WILLIAM GOLDMAN

20 ___ _____

_____

_____

_____

_____

20 ___ _____

_____

_____

_____

_____

20 ___ _____

_____

_____

_____

_____

20 ___ _____

_____

_____

_____

_____

20 ___ _____

_____

_____

_____

_____

JUNE 8

"We are all in the gutter, but some of us are looking at the stars."

20 ___ _____
_____
_____
_____

20 ___ _____
_____
_____
_____

20 ___ _____
_____
_____
_____

20 ___ _____
_____
_____
_____

20 ___ _____
_____
_____
_____

JUNE 9

"It took me fifteen years to discover I had no talent for writing, but I couldn't give it up, because by that time I was too famous."

—Robert Benchley

20 ___ _____

_____

_____

_____

_____

20 ___ _____

_____

_____

_____

_____

20 ___ _____

_____

_____

_____

_____

20 ___ _____

_____

_____

_____

_____

20 ___ _____

_____

_____

_____

_____

JUNE 10

"You've got to be honest; if you can fake that, you've got it made."

—GEORGE BURNS

20 ___ _____

_____

_____

_____

_____

20 ___ _____

_____

_____

_____

_____

20 ___ _____

_____

_____

_____

_____

20 ___ _____

_____

_____

_____

_____

20 ___ _____

_____

_____

_____

_____

JUNE 11

"A verbal contract is not worth the paper it's written on."

—SAMUEL GOLDWYN

20 ___

_____

_____

_____

_____

20 ___

_____

_____

_____

_____

20 ___

_____

_____

_____

_____

20 ___

_____

_____

_____

_____

20 ___

_____

_____

_____

_____

JUNE 12

"It is sometimes an appropriate response to reality to go insane."

—PHILIP K. DICK

20 ___ _____

_____

_____

_____

_____

20 ___ _____

_____

_____

_____

_____

20 ___ _____

_____

_____

_____

_____

20 ___ _____

_____

_____

_____

_____

20 ___ _____

_____

_____

_____

_____

JUNE 13 ·

"I really didn't say everything I said."

—YOGI BERRA

20 ___ _____

_____

_____

_____

20 ___ _____

_____

_____

_____

20 ___ _____

_____

_____

_____

20 ___ _____

_____

_____

_____

20 ___ _____

_____

_____

_____

JUNE 14

"I believe in getting into hot water. I think it keeps you clean."

—G.K. CHESTERTON

20 __ _____

_____

_____

_____

_____

20 __ _____

_____

_____

_____

_____

20 __ _____

_____

_____

_____

_____

20 __ _____

_____

_____

_____

_____

20 __ _____

_____

_____

_____

_____

JUNE 15

"If you want to see a comic strip, you should see me in the shower."

—GROUCHO MARX

20 ___ _____

_____

_____

_____

20 ___ _____

_____

_____

_____

20 ___ _____

_____

_____

_____

20 ___ _____

_____

_____

_____

20 ___ _____

_____

_____

_____

JUNE 16

"Roses are red, Violets are blue. I'm schizophrenic, and so am I."

—Oscar Levant

20 ___ _____

_____

_____

_____

20 ___ _____

_____

_____

_____

20 ___ _____

_____

_____

_____

20 ___ _____

_____

_____

_____

20 ___ _____

_____

_____

_____

JUNE 17

"Be thankful we're not getting all the government we're paying for."

—WILL ROGERS

20 ___ _____

_____

_____

_____

_____

20 ___ _____

_____

_____

_____

_____

20 ___ _____

_____

_____

_____

_____

20 ___ _____

_____

_____

_____

_____

20 ___ _____

_____

_____

_____

_____

JUNE 18

"Always borrow money from a pessimist. He won't expect it back."

—OSCAR WILDE

20 ___ _____

_____

_____

_____

_____

20 ___ _____

_____

_____

_____

_____

20 ___ _____

_____

_____

_____

_____

20 ___ _____

_____

_____

_____

_____

20 ___ _____

_____

_____

_____

_____

JUNE 19

"Do not argue with an idiot. He will drag you down to his level then beat you with experience."

20 ___ _____

_____

_____

_____

_____

20 ___ _____

_____

_____

_____

_____

20 ___ _____

_____

_____

_____

_____

20 ___ _____

_____

_____

_____

_____

20 ___ _____

_____

_____

_____

_____

JUNE 20

"I do benefits for all religions. I'd hate to blow the hereafter on a technicality."

—BOB HOPE

20 ___ _____

_____

_____

_____

_____

20 ___ _____

_____

_____

_____

_____

20 ___ _____

_____

_____

_____

_____

20 ___ _____

_____

_____

_____

_____

20 ___ _____

_____

_____

_____

_____

JUNE 21

"When I'm good I'm very, very good, but when I'm bad, I'm better."

—MAE WEST

20 _____ _____

_____

_____

_____

_____

20 _____ _____

_____

_____

_____

_____

20 _____ _____

_____

_____

_____

_____

20 _____ _____

_____

_____

_____

_____

20 _____ _____

_____

_____

_____

_____

JUNE 22

"Outside of a dog, a book is man's best friend. Inside of a dog, it's too dark to read."

—GROUCHO MARX

20 ___ _____

_____

_____

_____

_____

20 ___ _____

_____

_____

_____

_____

20 ___ _____

_____

_____

_____

_____

20 ___ _____

_____

_____

_____

_____

20 ___ _____

_____

_____

_____

_____

JUNE 23

"I can't understand why I flunked American history. When I was a kid there was so little of it."

20 __

_____

_____

_____

_____

20 __

_____

_____

_____

_____

20 __

_____

_____

_____

_____

20 __

_____

_____

_____

_____

20 __

_____

_____

_____

_____

JUNE 24

"Coffee isn't my cup of tea."

—SAMUEL GOLDWYN

20 __ _____

_____

_____

_____

20 __ _____

_____

_____

_____

20 __ _____

_____

_____

_____

20 __ _____

_____

_____

_____

20 __ _____

_____

_____

_____

JUNE 25

"Drawing on my fine command of the language, I said nothing."

—ROBERT BENCHLEY

20 ___ _____

_____

_____

_____

20 ___ _____

_____

_____

_____

20 ___ _____

_____

_____

_____

20 ___ _____

_____

_____

_____

20 ___ _____

_____

_____

_____

JUNE 26

"The person who writes for fools is always sure of a large audience."

—ARTHUR SHOPENHAUER

20 ___ _____

_____

_____

_____

_____

20 ___ _____

_____

_____

_____

_____

20 ___ _____

_____

_____

_____

_____

20 ___ _____

_____

_____

_____

_____

20 ___ _____

_____

_____

_____

_____

JUNE 27

"If you steal from one author, it's plagiarism;
If you steal from many, it's research."

—WILSON MIZNER

20 ___ _____

_____

_____

_____

20 ___ _____

_____

_____

_____

20 ___ _____

_____

_____

_____

20 ___ _____

_____

_____

_____

20 ___ _____

_____

_____

_____

JUNE 28

"Art, like morality, consists in drawing the line somewhere."

—G.K. CHESTERTON

20 ___ _____

_____

_____

_____

_____

20 ___ _____

_____

_____

_____

_____

20 ___ _____

_____

_____

_____

_____

20 ___ _____

_____

_____

_____

_____

20 ___ _____

_____

_____

_____

_____

JUNE 29

"I don't care what is written about me as long as it isn't true."

—KATHERINE HEPBURN

20 __ _____

_____

_____

_____

_____

20 __ _____

_____

_____

_____

_____

20 __ _____

_____

_____

_____

_____

20 __ _____

_____

_____

_____

_____

20 __ _____

_____

_____

_____

_____

JUNE 30

"A bargain is something you don't need at a price you can't resist."

—FRANKLIN JONES

20 ___ _____

_____

_____

_____

_____

20 ___ _____

_____

_____

_____

_____

20 ___ _____

_____

_____

_____

_____

20 ___ _____

_____

_____

_____

_____

20 ___ _____

_____

_____

_____

_____

JULY 1

"Don't cry because it's over, smile because it happened."

–DR. SEUSS

20 ___

_____

_____

_____

_____

20 ___

_____

_____

_____

_____

20 ___

_____

_____

_____

_____

20 ___

_____

_____

_____

_____

20 ___

_____

_____

_____

_____

JULY 2

"Those who are easily shocked should be shocked more often."

—MAE WEST

20 ___ _____

_____

_____

_____

_____

20 ___ _____

_____

_____

_____

_____

20 ___ _____

_____

_____

_____

20 ___ _____

_____

_____

_____

20 ___ _____

_____

_____

_____

JULY 3

"Imperfection is beauty, madness is genius and it's better to be absolutely ridiculous than absolutely boring."

—MARILYN MONROE

20 ___ _____

_____

_____

_____

_____

20 ___ _____

_____

_____

_____

_____

20 ___ _____

_____

_____

_____

_____

20 ___ _____

_____

_____

_____

_____

20 ___ _____

_____

_____

_____

_____

JULY 4

"I have found the paradox, that if you love until it hurts, there can be no more hurt, only more love."

—MOTHER TERESA

20 ___

_____

_____

_____

_____

20 ___

_____

_____

_____

_____

20 ___

_____

_____

_____

_____

20 ___

_____

_____

_____

_____

20 ___

_____

_____

_____

_____

JULY 5

"It is better to be hated for what you are than to be loved for what you are not."

—ANDRE GIDE

20 ___ _____

_____

_____

_____

_____

20 ___ _____

_____

_____

_____

_____

20 ___ _____

_____

_____

_____

_____

20 ___ _____

_____

_____

_____

_____

20 ___ _____

_____

_____

_____

_____

JULY 6

"Always do what you are afraid to do."

—RALPH WALDO EMERSON

20 ___ _____

_____

_____

_____

20 ___ _____

_____

_____

_____

20 ___ _____

_____

_____

_____

20 ___ _____

_____

_____

_____

20 ___ _____

_____

_____

_____

JULY 7

"If at first you don't succeed, try, try again. Then quit. No use being a damn fool about it."

—W.C. FIELDS

20 ___ _____

_____

_____

_____

20 ___ _____

_____

_____

_____

20 ___ _____

_____

_____

_____

20 ___ _____

_____

_____

_____

20 ___ _____

_____

_____

_____

JULY 8

20 ___

20 ___

20 ___

20 ___

20 ___

JULY 9

"There is no such thing as a moral or an immoral book. Books are well written, or badly written. That is all."

—OSCAR WILDE

20 ___

_____

20 ___

_____

20 ___

_____

20 ___

_____

20 ___

_____

JULY 10

"Of course it is happening inside your head, Harry, but why on earth should that mean that it is not real?"

20 ___

_____

20 ___

_____

20 ___

_____

20 ___

_____

20 ___

_____

JULY 11

"We are who we pretend to be, so we must be very careful about what we pretend to be."

—KURT VONNEGUT

20 ___

_____

_____

_____

_____

20 ___

_____

_____

_____

_____

20 ___

_____

_____

_____

_____

20 ___

_____

_____

_____

_____

20 ___

_____

_____

_____

_____

JULY 12

"Never doubt that a small group of thoughtful, committed citizens can change the world. Indeed, it's the only thing that ever has."

—MARGARET MEAD

20 ___ _____

_____

_____

_____

_____

20 ___ _____

_____

_____

_____

_____

20 ___ _____

_____

_____

_____

_____

20 ___ _____

_____

_____

_____

_____

20 ___ _____

_____

_____

_____

_____

JULY 13

"Men occasionally stumble over the truth, but most of them pick themselves up and hurry off as if nothing ever happened."

—WINSTON CHURCHILL

20 ___ _____

_____

_____

_____

_____

20 ___ _____

_____

_____

_____

_____

20 ___ _____

_____

_____

_____

20 ___ _____

_____

_____

_____

_____

20 ___ _____

_____

_____

_____

_____

JULY 14

"Being a woman is a terribly difficult task, since it consists principally in dealing with men."

—JOSEPH CONRAD

20 ___ _____

_____

_____

_____

_____

20 ___ _____

_____

_____

_____

_____

20 ___ _____

_____

_____

_____

_____

20 ___ _____

_____

_____

_____

_____

20 ___ _____

_____

_____

_____

_____

JULY 15

"Great spirits have always encountered violent opposition from mediocre minds."

—ALBERT EINSTEIN

20 ___ _____

_____

_____

_____

20 ___ _____

_____

_____

_____

20 ___ _____

_____

_____

_____

20 ___ _____

_____

_____

_____

20 ___ _____

_____

_____

_____

JULY 16

"It isn't what I do, but how I do it. It isn't what I say, but how I say it, and how I look when I do it and say it."

—MAE WEST

20 ___

_____

_____

_____

_____

20 ___

_____

_____

_____

_____

20 ___

_____

_____

_____

_____

20 ___

_____

_____

_____

_____

20 ___

_____

_____

_____

_____

JULY 17

"We have to dare to be ourselves, however frightening or strange that self may prove to be."

—MAY SARTON

20 ___

_____

20 ___

_____

20 ___

_____

20 ___

_____

20 ___

_____

JULY 18

"I am not young enough to know everything."

—OSCAR WILDE

20 ___

_____

_____

_____

_____

_____

20 ___

_____

_____

_____

_____

_____

20 ___

_____

_____

_____

_____

_____

20 ___

_____

_____

_____

_____

_____

20 ___

_____

_____

_____

_____

_____

JULY 19

"There are three types of lies -- lies, damn lies, and statistics."

—MARK TWAIN

20 ___ _____

_____

_____

_____

_____

20 ___ _____

_____

_____

_____

_____

20 ___ _____

_____

_____

_____

_____

20 ___ _____

_____

_____

_____

_____

20 ___ _____

_____

_____

_____

_____

JULY 20

"The saddest aspect of life right now is that science gathers knowledge faster than society gathers wisdom."

—Isaac Asimov

20 ___ _____

_____

_____

_____

_____

20 ___ _____

_____

_____

_____

_____

20 ___ _____

_____

_____

_____

_____

20 ___ _____

_____

_____

_____

_____

20 ___ _____

_____

_____

_____

_____

JULY 21

"The books that the world calls immoral are books that show the world its own shame."

—OSCAR WILDE

20 ___ _____

_____

_____

_____

_____

20 ___ _____

_____

_____

_____

_____

20 ___ _____

_____

_____

_____

_____

20 ___ _____

_____

_____

_____

_____

20 ___ _____

_____

_____

_____

_____

JULY 22

"If cats looked like frogs we'd realize what nasty, cruel little bastards they are. Style. That's what people remember."

—TERRY PRATCHETT

20 ___

_____

20 ___

_____

20 ___

_____

20 ___

_____

20 ___

_____

JULY 23

"Love is a fire. But whether it is going to warm your hearth or burn down your house, you can never tell."

—JOAN CRAWFORD

20 ___

_____

_____

_____

_____

20 ___

_____

_____

_____

_____

20 ___

_____

_____

_____

_____

20 ___

_____

_____

_____

_____

20 ___

_____

_____

_____

_____

JULY 24

"I'm the one that has to die when it's time for me to die, so let me live my life the way I want to."

—JIMI HENDRIX

20 ___

_____

20 ___

_____

20 ___

_____

20 ___

_____

20 ___

_____

JULY 25

"It is the mark of an educated mind to be able to entertain a thought without accepting it."

—ARISTOTLE

20 ___

_____

_____

_____

_____

20 ___

_____

_____

_____

_____

20 ___

_____

_____

_____

_____

20 ___

_____

_____

_____

_____

20 ___

_____

_____

_____

_____

JULY 26

"Do one thing every day that scares you."

—ELEANOR ROOSEVELT

20 ___ _____

_____

_____

_____

20 ___ _____

_____

_____

_____

20 ___ _____

_____

_____

_____

20 ___ _____

_____

_____

_____

20 ___ _____

_____

_____

_____

JULY 27

"The first time someone shows you who they are, believe them."

—MAYA ANGELOU

20 ___ _____

_____

_____

_____

_____

20 ___ _____

_____

_____

_____

_____

20 ___ _____

_____

_____

_____

_____

20 ___ _____

_____

_____

_____

_____

20 ___ _____

_____

_____

_____

_____

JULY 28

"I became insane, with long intervals of horrible sanity."

—EDGAR ALLEN POE

20 __ _____

_____

_____

_____

20 __ _____

_____

_____

_____

20 __ _____

_____

_____

_____

20 __ _____

_____

_____

_____

20 __ _____

_____

_____

_____

JULY 29

"Be kind, for everyone you meet is fighting a hard battle."

—PLATO

20 ___ _____

_____

_____

_____

20 ___ _____

_____

_____

_____

20 ___ _____

_____

_____

_____

20 ___ _____

_____

_____

_____

20 ___ _____

_____

_____

_____

JULY 30

"Do what you feel in your heart to be right — for you'll be criticized anyway."

—ELEANOR ROOSEVELT

20 ___ _____

_____

_____

_____

_____

20 ___ _____

_____

_____

_____

_____

20 ___ _____

_____

_____

_____

_____

20 ___ _____

_____

_____

_____

_____

20 ___ _____

_____

_____

_____

_____

JULY 31

"Poets have been mysteriously silent on the subject of cheese."

—G.K. CHESTERTON

20 ___ _____

_____

_____

_____

_____

20 ___ _____

_____

_____

_____

_____

20 ___ _____

_____

_____

_____

_____

20 ___ _____

_____

_____

_____

_____

20 ___ _____

_____

_____

_____

_____

AUGUST 1

"Always do what is right. It will gratify half of mankind and astound the other."

—MARK TWAIN

20 __ _____

_____

_____

_____

_____

20 __ _____

_____

_____

_____

_____

20 __ _____

_____

_____

_____

_____

20 __ _____

_____

_____

_____

_____

20 __ _____

_____

_____

_____

_____

AUGUST 2

"Right now I'm having amnesia and déjà vu at the same time. I think I've forgotten this before."

—STEVEN WRIGHT

20 ___ _____

_____

_____

_____

20 ___ _____

_____

_____

_____

20 ___ _____

_____

_____

_____

20 ___ _____

_____

_____

_____

20 ___ _____

_____

_____

_____

AUGUST 3

"Worry is a waste of imagination."

—Anonymous

20 ___ _____

_____

_____

_____

_____

20 ___ _____

_____

_____

_____

_____

20 ___ _____

_____

_____

_____

_____

20 ___ _____

_____

_____

_____

_____

20 ___ _____

_____

_____

_____

_____

AUGUST 4

"The only thing necessary for the triumph of evil is for good men to do nothing."

—EDMUND BURKE

20 ___

_____

_____

_____

_____

20 ___

_____

_____

_____

_____

20 ___

_____

_____

_____

_____

20 ___

_____

_____

_____

_____

20 ___

_____

_____

_____

_____

AUGUST 5

"Man is the only creature who refuses to be what he is."

—ALBERT CAMUS

20 ___ _____

_____

_____

_____

_____

20 ___ _____

_____

_____

_____

_____

20 ___ _____

_____

_____

_____

_____

20 ___ _____

_____

_____

_____

20 ___ _____

_____

_____

_____

_____

AUGUST 6

"Life's hard. It's even harder when you're stupid."

—JOHN WAYNE

20 ___ _____

_____

_____

_____

20 ___ _____

_____

_____

_____

20 ___ _____

_____

_____

_____

20 ___ _____

_____

_____

_____

20 ___ _____

_____

_____

_____

AUGUST 7

"A life spent making mistakes is not only more honorable, but more useful than a life spent doing nothing."

—GEORGE BERNARD SHAW

20 ___ _____

_____

_____

_____

20 ___ _____

_____

_____

_____

20 ___ _____

_____

_____

_____

20 ___ _____

_____

_____

_____

20 ___ _____

_____

_____

_____

AUGUST 8

"Every child is an artist. The problem is how to remain an artist once he grows up."

20 ___ _____

_____

_____

_____

_____

20 ___ _____

_____

_____

_____

_____

20 ___ _____

_____

_____

_____

_____

20 ___ _____

_____

_____

_____

_____

20 ___ _____

_____

_____

_____

_____

AUGUST 9

"The world as we have created it is a process of our thinking. It cannot be changed without changing our thinking."

—ALBERT EINSTEIN

20 ___

_____

20 ___

_____

20 ___

_____

20 ___

_____

20 ___

_____

AUGUST 10

"Unless someone like you cares a whole awful lot, nothing is going to get better. It's not."

20 ___ _____

_____

_____

_____

20 ___ _____

_____

_____

_____

20 ___ _____

_____

_____

_____

20 ___ _____

_____

_____

_____

20 ___ _____

_____

_____

_____

AUGUST 11

"Always do sober what you said you'd do drunk. That will teach you to keep your mouth shut."

—ERNEST HEMINGWAY

20 ___ _____

_____

_____

_____

_____

20 ___ _____

_____

_____

_____

_____

20 ___ _____

_____

_____

_____

_____

20 ___ _____

_____

_____

_____

_____

20 ___ _____

_____

_____

_____

_____

AUGUST 12

"I always arrive late at the office, but I make up for it by leaving early."

—CHARLES LAMB

20 ___ _____

_____

_____

_____

20 ___ _____

_____

_____

_____

20 ___ _____

_____

_____

_____

20 ___ _____

_____

_____

_____

20 ___ _____

_____

_____

_____

AUGUST 13

"Everyone should be able to do one card trick, tell two jokes, and recite three poems, in case they are ever trapped in an elevator."

—LEMONY SNICKET

20 ___ _____

_____

_____

_____

20 ___ _____

_____

_____

_____

20 ___ _____

_____

_____

_____

20 ___ _____

_____

_____

_____

20 ___ _____

_____

_____

_____

AUGUST 14

"History will be kind to me for I intend to write it."

—WINSTON CHURCHILL

20 ___ _____

_____

_____

_____

20 ___ _____

_____

_____

_____

20 ___ _____

_____

_____

_____

20 ___ _____

_____

_____

_____

20 ___ _____

_____

_____

_____

AUGUST 15

"Life is pain, highness. Anyone who tells you differently is selling something."

—WILLIAM GOLDMAN

20 ___

_____

20 ___

_____

20 ___

_____

20 ___

_____

20 ___

_____

AUGUST 16

"Words are, of course, the most powerful drug used by mankind."

—RUDYARD KIPLING

20 ___ _____

_____

_____

_____

_____

20 ___ _____

_____

_____

_____

_____

20 ___ _____

_____

_____

_____

_____

20 ___ _____

_____

_____

_____

_____

20 ___ _____

_____

_____

_____

_____

AUGUST 17

"I believe the only way to get through this life is laughing, mostly at myself."

—SHANNON HALE

20 ___ _____

_____

_____

_____

20 ___ _____

_____

_____

_____

20 ___ _____

_____

_____

_____

20 ___ _____

_____

_____

_____

20 ___ _____

_____

_____

_____

AUGUST 18

"You live but once; you might as well be amusing."

20 ___ _____

_____
_____
_____
_____

20 ___ _____

_____
_____
_____
_____

20 ___ _____

_____
_____
_____
_____

20 ___ _____

_____
_____
_____
_____

20 ___ _____

_____
_____
_____
_____

AUGUST 19

"Don't part with your illusions. When they are gone you may still exist, but you have ceased to live."

—MARK TWAIN

20 ___ _____

_____

_____

_____

_____

20 ___ _____

_____

_____

_____

_____

20 ___ _____

_____

_____

_____

_____

20 ___ _____

_____

_____

_____

_____

20 ___ _____

_____

_____

_____

_____

AUGUST 20

"Cats are intended to teach us that not everything in nature has a purpose."

—GARRISON KEILLOR

20 ___

_____

_____

_____

_____

20 ___

_____

_____

_____

_____

20 ___

_____

_____

_____

_____

20 ___

_____

_____

_____

_____

20 ___

_____

_____

_____

_____

AUGUST 21

"Sometimes I can hear my bones straining under the weight of all the lives I'm not living."

—Jonathan Safran Foer

20 ___ _____

_____

_____

_____

_____

20 ___ _____

_____

_____

_____

_____

20 ___ _____

_____

_____

_____

_____

20 ___ _____

_____

_____

_____

_____

20 ___ _____

_____

_____

_____

_____

AUGUST 22

"This is not a novel to be tossed aside lightly. It should be thrown with great force."

—DOROTHY PARKER

20 ___ _____

_____

_____

_____

20 ___ _____

_____

_____

_____

20 ___ _____

_____

_____

_____

20 ___ _____

_____

_____

_____

20 ___ _____

_____

_____

_____

AUGUST 23

"You will never live if you are looking for the meaning of life."

—ALBERT CAMUS

20 ___ _____

_____

_____

_____

_____

20 ___ _____

_____

_____

_____

_____

20 ___ _____

_____

_____

_____

_____

20 ___ _____

_____

_____

_____

_____

20 ___ _____

_____

_____

_____

_____

AUGUST 24

"In a time of deceit telling the truth is a revolutionary act."

—George Orwell

20 ___

20 ___

20 ___

20 ___

20 ___

AUGUST 25

"Everyone thinks of changing the world, but no one thinks of changing himself."

—LEO TOLSTOY

20 ___ _____

_____

_____

_____

20 ___ _____

_____

_____

_____

20 ___ _____

_____

_____

_____

20 ___ _____

_____

_____

_____

20 ___ _____

_____

_____

_____

AUGUST 26

"All the darkness in the world can't extinguish the light from a single candle."

—St. Francis of Assisi

20 ___

20 ___

20 ___

20 ___

20 ___

AUGUST 27

"Do not fear to be eccentric in opinion, for every opinion now accepted was once eccentric."

—BERTRAND RUSSELL

20 ___ _____

_____

_____

_____

_____

20 ___ _____

_____

_____

_____

_____

20 ___ _____

_____

_____

_____

_____

20 ___ _____

_____

_____

_____

_____

20 ___ _____

_____

_____

_____

_____

AUGUST 28

"My tastes are simple: I am easily satisfied with the best."

—WINSTON CHURCHILL

20 ___ _____

_____

_____

_____

_____

20 ___ _____

_____

_____

_____

_____

20 ___ _____

_____

_____

_____

_____

20 ___ _____

_____

_____

_____

_____

20 ___ _____

_____

_____

_____

_____

AUGUST 29

"The problem with designing something completely foolproof is to underestimate the ingenuity of a complete fool."

—DOUGLAS ADAMS

20 ___ _____

_____

_____

_____

_____

20 ___ _____

_____

_____

_____

_____

20 ___ _____

_____

_____

_____

_____

20 ___ _____

_____

_____

_____

_____

20 ___ _____

_____

_____

_____

_____

AUGUST 30

"It's not worth doing something unless someone, somewhere, would much rather you weren't doing it."

—TERRY PRATCHETT

20 ___ _____

_____

_____

_____

_____

20 ___ _____

_____

_____

_____

_____

20 ___ _____

_____

_____

_____

20 ___ _____

_____

_____

_____

_____

20 ___ _____

_____

_____

_____

_____

AUGUST 31

"A cynic is a man who knows the price of everything, and the value of nothing."

20 ___ _____

_____

_____

_____

20 ___ _____

_____

_____

_____

20 ___ _____

_____

_____

_____

20 ___ _____

_____

_____

_____

20 ___ _____

_____

_____

_____

SEPTEMBER 1

"I hate to advocate drugs, alcohol, violence, or insanity to anyone, but they've always worked for me."

—HUNTER S. THOMAS

20 ___ _____

_____

_____

_____

20 ___ _____

_____

_____

_____

20 ___ _____

_____

_____

_____

20 ___ _____

_____

_____

_____

20 ___ _____

_____

_____

_____

SEPTEMBER 2

"Name the greatest of all inventors. Accident."

—MARK TWAIN

20 ___ _____

_____

_____

_____

_____

20 ___ _____

_____

_____

_____

_____

20 ___ _____

_____

_____

_____

_____

20 ___ _____

_____

_____

_____

_____

20 ___ _____

_____

_____

_____

_____

SEPTEMBER 3

"The most wasted of all days is one without laughter."

—EE CUMMINGS

20 __ _____

_____

_____

_____

20 __ _____

_____

_____

_____

20 __ _____

_____

_____

_____

20 __ _____

_____

_____

_____

20 __ _____

_____

_____

_____

SEPTEMBER 4

"Never interrupt your enemy when he is making a mistake."

—NAPOLEON BONAPARTE

20 ___ _____

_____

_____

_____

20 ___ _____

_____

_____

_____

20 ___ _____

_____

_____

_____

20 ___ _____

_____

_____

_____

20 ___ _____

_____

_____

_____

SEPTEMBER 5

"Nobody realizes that some people expend tremendous energy merely to be normal."

—ALBERT CAMUS

20 ___ _____

_____

_____

_____

20 ___ _____

_____

_____

_____

20 ___ _____

_____

_____

_____

20 ___ _____

_____

_____

_____

20 ___ _____

_____

_____

_____

SEPTEMBER 6

*"If you don't read the newspaper, you're uninformed. If you read the
newspaper, you're mis-informed."*

—MARK TWAIN

20 ___ _____

_____

_____

_____

20 ___ _____

_____

_____

_____

20 ___ _____

_____

_____

_____

20 ___ _____

_____

_____

_____

20 ___ _____

_____

_____

_____

SEPTEMBER 7

"In ancient times cats were worshipped as gods; they have not forgotten this."

—TERRY PRATCHETT

20 ___

_____

_____

_____

_____

20 ___

_____

_____

_____

_____

20 ___

_____

_____

_____

_____

20 ___

_____

_____

_____

_____

20 ___

_____

_____

_____

_____

SEPTEMBER 8

"Freedom is not worth having if it does not include the freedom to make mistakes."

—MAHATMA GANDHI

20 ___ _____

_____

_____

_____

_____

20 ___ _____

_____

_____

_____

_____

20 ___ _____

_____

_____

_____

_____

20 ___ _____

_____

_____

_____

_____

20 ___ _____

_____

_____

_____

_____

SEPTEMBER 9

"Without deviation from the norm, progress is not possible."

—FRANK ZAPPA

20 __ _____

_____

_____

_____

_____

20 __ _____

_____

_____

_____

_____

20 __ _____

_____

_____

_____

_____

20 __ _____

_____

_____

_____

_____

20 __ _____

_____

_____

_____

_____

SEPTEMBER 10

"Better to be hurt by the truth than comforted with a lie."

—KHALED HOSSEINI

20 ___ _____

_____

_____

_____

20 ___ _____

_____

_____

_____

20 ___ _____

_____

_____

_____

20 ___ _____

_____

_____

_____

20 ___ _____

_____

_____

_____

SEPTEMBER 11

"I'm killing time while I wait for life to shower me with meaning and happiness."

—BILL WATTERSON

20 ___ _____

_____

_____

_____

20 ___ _____

_____

_____

_____

20 ___ _____

_____

_____

_____

20 ___ _____

_____

_____

_____

20 ___ _____

_____

_____

_____

SEPTEMBER 12

"I don't want to go to heaven. None of my friends are there."

—OSCAR WILDE

20 __ _____

_____

_____

_____

20 __ _____

_____

_____

_____

20 __ _____

_____

_____

_____

20 __ _____

_____

_____

_____

20 __ _____

_____

_____

_____

SEPTEMBER 13

"Life isn't about finding yourself. Life is about creating yourself."

—GEORGE BERNARD SHAW

20 ___ _____

_____

_____

_____

20 ___ _____

_____

_____

_____

20 ___ _____

_____

_____

_____

20 ___ _____

_____

_____

_____

20 ___ _____

_____

_____

_____

SEPTEMBER 14

"The truth will set you free, but first it will piss you off."

—GLORIA STEINEM

20 ___ _____

_____

_____

_____

_____

20 ___ _____

_____

_____

_____

_____

20 ___ _____

_____

_____

_____

_____

20 ___ _____

_____

_____

_____

_____

20 ___ _____

_____

_____

_____

_____

SEPTEMBER 15

"I tell you, we are here on Earth to fart around, and don't let anybody tell you different."

—KURT VONNEGUT

20 ___ _____

_____

_____

_____

20 ___ _____

_____

_____

_____

20 ___ _____

_____

_____

_____

20 ___ _____

_____

_____

_____

20 ___ _____

_____

_____

_____

SEPTEMBER 16

"An expert is a person who has made all the mistakes that can be made in a very narrow field."

—Niels Bohr

20 ___ _____

_____
_____
_____
_____

20 ___ _____

_____
_____
_____
_____

20 ___ _____

_____
_____
_____
_____

20 ___ _____

_____
_____
_____
_____

20 ___ _____

_____
_____
_____
_____

SEPTEMBER 17

"It is impossible to live without failing at something, unless you live so cautiously that you might as well not have lived at all."

—BILL WATTERSON

20 ___

_____

_____

_____

_____

20 ___

_____

_____

_____

_____

20 ___

_____

_____

_____

_____

20 ___

_____

_____

_____

_____

20 ___

_____

_____

_____

_____

SEPTEMBER 18

"Disbelief in magic can force a poor soul into believing in government and business."

—TOM ROBBINS

20 ___ _____

_____

_____

_____

_____

20 ___ _____

_____

_____

_____

_____

20 ___ _____

_____

_____

_____

_____

20 ___ _____

_____

_____

_____

_____

20 ___ _____

_____

_____

_____

_____

SEPTEMBER 19

"A learning experience is one of those things that says, 'You know that thing you just did? Don't do that."

—Douglas Adams

20 ___ _____

_____

_____

_____

20 ___ _____

_____

_____

_____

20 ___ _____

_____

_____

_____

20 ___ _____

_____

_____

_____

20 ___ _____

_____

_____

_____

SEPTEMBER 20

"You can only be young once. But you can always be immature."

—DAVE BARRY

20 ___ _____

_____

_____

_____

_____

20 ___ _____

_____

_____

_____

_____

20 ___ _____

_____

_____

_____

_____

20 ___ _____

_____

_____

_____

_____

20 ___ _____

_____

_____

_____

_____

SEPTEMBER 21

"Live to the point of tears."

—ALBERT CAMUS

20 ___ _____

_____

_____

_____

20 ___ _____

_____

_____

_____

20 ___ _____

_____

_____

_____

20 ___ _____

_____

_____

_____

20 ___ _____

_____

_____

_____

SEPTEMBER 22

"Life doesn't imitate art, it imitates bad television."

—WOODY ALLEN

20 ___ _____

_____

_____

_____

_____

20 ___ _____

_____

_____

_____

_____

20 ___ _____

_____

_____

_____

_____

20 ___ _____

_____

_____

_____

_____

20 ___ _____

_____

_____

_____

_____

SEPTEMBER 23

"You wouldn't worry so much about what others think of you if you realized how seldom they do."

—ELEANOR ROOSEVELT

20 ___ _____

_____

_____

_____

20 ___ _____

_____

_____

_____

20 ___ _____

_____

_____

_____

20 ___ _____

_____

_____

_____

20 ___ _____

_____

_____

_____

SEPTEMBER 24

"I don't know much about being a millionaire, but I'll bet I'd be darling at it."

—DOROTHY PARKER

20 ___ _____

_____

_____

_____

_____

20 ___ _____

_____

_____

_____

_____

20 ___ _____

_____

_____

_____

_____

20 ___ _____

_____

_____

_____

_____

20 ___ _____

_____

_____

_____

_____

SEPTEMBER 25

"Man is least himself when he talks in his own person. Give him a mask, and he will tell you the truth."

—OSCAR WILDE

20 ___ _____

_____

_____

_____

20 ___ _____

_____

_____

_____

20 ___ _____

_____

_____

_____

20 ___ _____

_____

_____

_____

20 ___ _____

_____

_____

_____

SEPTEMBER 26

"Never attribute to malice that which can be adequately explained by stupidity."

—ROBERT A. HEINLEIN

20 ____

20 ____

20 ____

20 ____

20 ____

SEPTEMBER 27

"Out on the edge you see all the kinds of things you can't see from the center."

—KURT VONNEGUT

20 ___

20 ___

20 ___

20 ___

20 ___

SEPTEMBER 28

"None of us really changes over time. We only become more fully what we are."

—ANNE RICE

20 ___ _____

_____

_____

_____

_____

20 ___ _____

_____

_____

_____

_____

20 ___ _____

_____

_____

_____

_____

20 ___ _____

_____

_____

_____

_____

20 ___ _____

_____

_____

_____

_____

SEPTEMBER 29

"For what do we live, but to make sport for our neighbors, and laugh at them in our turn."

—JANE AUSTEN

20 ___

_____

_____

_____

_____

20 ___

_____

_____

_____

_____

20 ___

_____

_____

_____

_____

20 ___

_____

_____

_____

_____

20 ___

_____

_____

_____

_____

SEPTEMBER 30

"Life is like riding a bicycle. To keep your balance, you must keep moving."

—ALBERT EINSTEIN

20 ___ _____

_____

_____

_____

20 ___ _____

_____

_____

_____

20 ___ _____

_____

_____

_____

20 ___ _____

_____

_____

_____

20 ___ _____

_____

_____

_____

OCTOBER 1

"Live in the present, remember the past, and fear not the future, for it doesn't exist and never shall. There is only now."

—CHRISTOPHER PAOLINI

20 ___ _____

_____

_____

_____

20 ___ _____

_____

_____

_____

20 ___ _____

_____

_____

_____

20 ___ _____

_____

_____

_____

20 ___ _____

_____

_____

_____

OCTOBER 2

"Life shrinks or expands in proportion to one's courage."

—ANAIS NIN

20 __ _____

_____

_____

_____

_____

20 __ _____

_____

_____

_____

_____

20 __ _____

_____

_____

_____

_____

20 __ _____

_____

_____

_____

_____

20 __ _____

_____

_____

_____

_____

OCTOBER 3

"If we could bottle up your luck, we'd have a weapon of mass destruction on our hands."

20 ___ _____

_____

_____

_____

20 ___ _____

_____

_____

_____

20 ___ _____

_____

_____

_____

20 ___ _____

_____

_____

_____

20 ___ _____

_____

_____

_____

OCTOBER 4

"Life's under no obligation to give us what we expect."

—MARGARET MITCHELL

20 ___

_____

_____

_____

_____

_____

20 ___

_____

_____

_____

_____

_____

20 ___

_____

_____

_____

_____

_____

20 ___

_____

_____

_____

_____

_____

20 ___

_____

_____

_____

_____

_____

OCTOBER 5

"The only way to get rid of temptation is to yield to it."

—OSCAR WILDE

20 ___ _____

_____

_____

_____

_____

20 ___ _____

_____

_____

_____

_____

20 ___ _____

_____

_____

_____

_____

20 ___ _____

_____

_____

_____

_____

20 ___ _____

_____

_____

_____

_____

OCTOBER 6

"I've had a perfectly wonderful evening, but this wasn't it."

—GROUCHO MARX

20 ___ _____

_____

_____

_____

20 ___ _____

_____

_____

_____

20 ___ _____

_____

_____

_____

20 ___ _____

_____

_____

_____

20 ___ _____

_____

_____

_____

OCTOBER 7

"If you think you are too small to make a difference,
try sleeping with a mosquito."

—DALAI LAMA XIV

20 ___ _____

20 ___ _____

20 ___ _____

20 ___ _____

20 ___ _____

OCTOBER 8

"The difference between fiction and reality?
Fiction has to make sense."

—TOM CLANCY

20 ___ _____

_____

_____

_____

_____

20 ___ _____

_____

_____

_____

_____

20 ___ _____

_____

_____

_____

_____

20 ___ _____

_____

_____

_____

_____

20 ___ _____

_____

_____

_____

_____

OCTOBER 9

"Any man who can drive safely while kissing a pretty girl is simply not giving the kiss the attention it deserves."

—ALBERT EINSTEIN

20 ___ _____

_____

_____

_____

20 ___ _____

_____

_____

_____

20 ___ _____

_____

_____

_____

20 ___ _____

_____

_____

_____

20 ___ _____

_____

_____

_____

OCTOBER 10

"Nearly all men can stand adversity, but if you want to test a man's character, give him power."

—ABRAHAM LINCOLN

20 ___ _____

_____

_____

_____

_____

20 ___ _____

_____

_____

_____

_____

20 ___ _____

_____

_____

_____

_____

20 ___ _____

_____

_____

_____

_____

20 ___ _____

_____

_____

_____

_____

OCTOBER 11

"Illegal aliens have always been a problem in the United States.
Ask any Indian."

—ROBERT ORBEN

20 ___ _____

_____

_____

_____

20 ___ _____

_____

_____

_____

20 ___ _____

_____

_____

_____

20 ___ _____

_____

_____

_____

20 ___ _____

_____

_____

_____

OCTOBER 12

"The surest sign that intelligent life exists elsewhere in the universe is that it has never tried to contact us."

—BILL WATTERSON

20 ___ _____

_____

_____

_____

_____

20 ___ _____

_____

_____

_____

_____

20 ___ _____

_____

_____

_____

_____

20 ___ _____

_____

_____

_____

_____

20 ___ _____

_____

_____

_____

_____

OCTOBER 13

"The greatness of a nation and its moral progress can be judged by the way its animals are treated."

—MAHATMA GANDHI

20 ___ _____

_____

_____

_____

_____

20 ___ _____

_____

_____

_____

_____

20 ___ _____

_____

_____

_____

_____

20 ___ _____

_____

_____

_____

_____

20 ___ _____

_____

_____

_____

_____

OCTOBER 14

"I know not with what weapons World War III will be fought,
but World War IV will be fought with sticks and stones."

—ALBERT EINSTEIN

20 ___ _____

_____

_____

_____

_____

20 ___ _____

_____

_____

_____

_____

20 ___ _____

_____

_____

_____

_____

20 ___ _____

_____

_____

_____

_____

20 ___ _____

_____

_____

_____

_____

OCTOBER 15

"Fiction is the truth inside the lie."

—STEPHEN KING

20 16 Today we finished our move. I am
stunned at the grace + blessings of God. A new
home + friends + family that made it happen. I am
also stunned at the depth of my selfishness. I still find
room to be irritable. SPEND MORE TIME IN HIS
PRESENCE!!

20 ___

20 ___

20 ___

20 ___

OCTOBER 16

"It's not denial. I'm just selective about the reality I accept."

—BILL WATTERSON

20 ___ _____

_____

_____

_____

_____

20 ___ _____

_____

_____

_____

_____

20 ___ _____

_____

_____

_____

_____

20 ___ _____

_____

_____

_____

_____

20 ___ _____

_____

_____

_____

_____

OCTOBER 17

"I wrote the story myself. It's about a girl who lost her reputation and never missed it."

—MAE WEST

20 ___ _____

_____

_____

_____

_____

20 ___ _____

_____

_____

_____

_____

20 ___ _____

_____

_____

_____

_____

20 ___ _____

_____

_____

_____

_____

20 ___ _____

_____

_____

_____

_____

OCTOBER 18

"Nothing is impossible, the word itself says 'I'm possible'!"

—AUDREY HEPBURN

20 ___ _____

_____

_____

_____

_____

20 ___ _____

_____

_____

_____

_____

20 ___ _____

_____

_____

_____

_____

20 ___ _____

_____

_____

_____

_____

20 ___ _____

_____

_____

_____

_____

OCTOBER 19

"One of the great things about books is sometimes there are some fantastic pictures."

—George W. Bush

20 ___ _____

_____

_____

_____

_____

20 ___ _____

_____

_____

_____

_____

20 ___ _____

_____

_____

_____

_____

20 ___ _____

_____

_____

_____

_____

20 ___ _____

_____

_____

_____

_____

OCTOBER 20

"Get your facts first, and then you can distort them as much as you please."

—MARK TWAIN

20 ___ _____

_____

_____

_____

_____

20 ___ _____

_____

_____

_____

_____

20 ___ _____

_____

_____

_____

_____

20 ___ _____

_____

_____

_____

_____

20 ___ _____

_____

_____

_____

_____

OCTOBER 21

"Fashion is a form of ugliness so intolerable that we have to alter it every six months."

—OSCAR WILDE

20 ___ _____

_____

_____

_____

20 ___ _____

_____

_____

_____

20 ___ _____

_____

_____

_____

20 ___ _____

_____

_____

_____

20 ___ _____

_____

_____

_____

OCTOBER 22

*"You have enemies? Good. That means you've stood up for
something sometime in your life."*

—WINSTON CHURCHILL

20 16   Rom. 7.24. I am so sick of this

20 __

20 __

20 __

20 __

OCTOBER 23

"I disapprove of what you say, but I will defend to the death your right to say it."

—Voltaire

20 ___ _____

_____

_____

_____

20 ___ _____

_____

_____

_____

20 ___ _____

_____

_____

_____

20 ___ _____

_____

_____

_____

20 ___ _____

_____

_____

_____

OCTOBER 24

"There are no good girls gone wrong - just bad girls found out."

—Mae West

20 ___ _____

_____

_____

_____

_____

20 ___ _____

_____

_____

_____

_____

20 ___ _____

_____

_____

_____

_____

20 ___ _____

_____

_____

_____

20 ___ _____

_____

_____

_____

_____

OCTOBER 25

"I did not attend his funeral, but I sent a nice letter saying I approved of it."

—MARK TWAIN

20 __ _____

_____

_____

_____

_____

20 __ _____

_____

_____

_____

_____

20 __ _____

_____

_____

_____

_____

20 __ _____

_____

_____

_____

_____

20 __ _____

_____

_____

_____

_____

OCTOBER 26

"I would believe only in a God that knows how to dance."

—FRIEDRICH WILHELM NIETZSCHE

20 ___ _____

_____

_____

_____

20 ___ _____

_____

_____

_____

20 ___ _____

_____

_____

_____

20 ___ _____

_____

_____

_____

20 ___ _____

_____

_____

_____

OCTOBER 27

"Tell the truth, or someone will tell it for you."

—STEPHANIE KLEIN

20 ___ _____

_____

_____

_____

_____

20 ___ _____

_____

_____

_____

_____

20 ___ _____

_____

_____

_____

_____

20 ___ _____

_____

_____

_____

_____

20 ___ _____

_____

_____

_____

_____

OCTOBER 28

"I suppose I'll have to add the force of gravity to my list of enemies."

—LEMONY SNICKET

20 ___ _____

_____

_____

_____

20 ___ _____

_____

_____

_____

20 ___ _____

_____

_____

_____

20 ___ _____

_____

_____

_____

20 ___ _____

_____

_____

_____

OCTOBER 29

"The trouble is if you don't spend your life yourself, other people spend it for you."

—PETER SHAFFER

20 ___ _____

_____

_____

_____

20 ___ _____

_____

_____

_____

20 ___ _____

_____

_____

_____

20 ___ _____

_____

_____

_____

20 ___ _____

_____

_____

_____

OCTOBER 30

"Tell me, what is it you plan to do with your one wild and precious life?"

—MARY OLIVER

20 ___ _____

_____

_____

_____

20 ___ _____

_____

_____

_____

20 ___ _____

_____

_____

_____

20 ___ _____

_____

_____

_____

20 ___ _____

_____

_____

_____

OCTOBER 31

"Halloween is the one night a year when girls can dress like a total slut and no other girls can say anything about it."

—LINDSAY LOHAN

20 ___ _____

_____

_____

_____

20 ___ _____

_____

_____

_____

20 ___ _____

_____

_____

_____

20 ___ _____

_____

_____

_____

20 ___ _____

_____

_____

_____

NOVEMBER 1

"Those are my principles, and if you don't like them...
well, I have others."

—GROUCHO MARX

20 ___ _____

_____

_____

_____

_____

20 ___ _____

_____

_____

_____

_____

20 ___ _____

_____

_____

_____

_____

20 ___ _____

_____

_____

_____

_____

20 ___ _____

_____

_____

_____

_____

NOVEMBER 2

"In the beginning there was nothing, which exploded."

—TERRY PRATCHETT

20 ___ _____

_____

_____

_____

20 ___ _____

_____

_____

_____

20 ___ _____

_____

_____

_____

20 ___ _____

_____

_____

_____

20 ___ _____

_____

_____

_____

NOVEMBER 3

"The things you own end up owning you."

—CHUCK PALAHNIUK

20 ___ _____

_____

_____

_____

20 ___ _____

_____

_____

_____

20 ___ _____

_____

_____

_____

20 ___ _____

_____

_____

_____

20 ___ _____

_____

_____

_____

NOVEMBER 4

"Remember: The time you feel lonely is the time you most need to be by yourself. Life's cruelest irony."

20 ___ _____

_____

_____

_____

20 ___ _____

_____

_____

_____

20 ___ _____

_____

_____

_____

20 ___ _____

_____

_____

_____

20 ___ _____

_____

_____

_____

NOVEMBER 5

"It is one of life's bitterest truths that bedtime so often arrives just when things are really getting interesting."

—LEMONY SNICKET

20 ___ _____

_____

_____

_____

20 ___ _____

_____

_____

_____

20 ___ _____

_____

_____

_____

20 ___ _____

_____

_____

_____

20 ___ _____

_____

_____

_____

NOVEMBER 6

"I don't go looking for trouble. Trouble usually finds me."

—J.K. ROWLING

20 ___ _____

_____

_____

_____

_____

20 ___ _____

_____

_____

_____

_____

20 ___ _____

_____

_____

_____

_____

20 ___ _____

_____

_____

_____

20 ___ _____

_____

_____

_____

_____

NOVEMBER 7

*"I don't mind living in a man's world,
as long as I can be a woman in it."*

—MARILYN MONROE

20 ___ _____

_____

_____

_____

_____

20 ___ _____

_____

_____

_____

_____

20 ___ _____

_____

_____

_____

_____

20 ___ _____

_____

_____

_____

_____

20 ___ _____

_____

_____

_____

_____

NOVEMBER 8

"I never forget a face, but in your case I'll be glad to make an exception."

—GROUCHO MARX

20 ___ _____

_____

_____

_____

_____

20 ___ _____

_____

_____

_____

_____

20 ___ _____

_____

_____

_____

_____

20 ___ _____

_____

_____

_____

_____

20 ___ _____

_____

_____

_____

_____

NOVEMBER 9

"If you can dream it, you can do it. Always remember that this whole thing was started with a dream and a mouse."

—WALT DISNEY

20 ___ _____

_____

_____

_____

_____

20 ___ _____

_____

_____

_____

_____

20 ___ _____

_____

_____

_____

_____

20 ___ _____

_____

_____

_____

_____

20 ___ _____

_____

_____

_____

_____

NOVEMBER 10

"Every saint has a past, and every sinner has a future."

—OSCAR WILDE

20 __ _____

_____

_____

_____

_____

20 __ _____

_____

_____

_____

_____

20 __ _____

_____

_____

_____

_____

20 __ _____

_____

_____

_____

_____

20 __ _____

_____

_____

_____

_____

NOVEMBER 11

"History doesn't repeat itself, but it does rhyme."

—MARK TWAIN

20 ___ _____

_____

_____

_____

20 ___ _____

_____

_____

_____

20 ___ _____

_____

_____

_____

20 ___ _____

_____

_____

_____

20 ___ _____

_____

_____

_____

NOVEMBER 12

"Someone who thinks death is the scariest thing doesn't know a thing about life."

—SUE MONK KIDD

20 ___ _____

_____

_____

_____

20 ___ _____

_____

_____

_____

20 ___ _____

_____

_____

_____

20 ___ _____

_____

_____

_____

20 ___ _____

_____

_____

_____

NOVEMBER 13

"Happiness makes up in height for what it lacks in length."

—ROBERT FROST

20 ___ _____

_____

_____

_____

_____

20 ___ _____

_____

_____

_____

_____

20 ___ _____

_____

_____

_____

_____

20 ___ _____

_____

_____

_____

_____

20 ___ _____

_____

_____

_____

_____

NOVEMBER 14

"The capacity for friendship is God's way of apologizing for our families."

—JAY MCINERNEY

20 __ _____

_____

_____

_____

_____

20 __ _____

_____

_____

_____

_____

20 __ _____

_____

_____

_____

_____

20 __ _____

_____

_____

_____

_____

20 __ _____

_____

_____

_____

_____

NOVEMBER 15

"I were two-faced, would I be wearing this one?"

—ABRAHAM LINCOLN

20 ___ _____

_____

_____

_____

20 ___ _____

_____

_____

_____

20 ___ _____

_____

_____

_____

20 ___ _____

_____

_____

_____

20 ___ _____

_____

_____

_____

NOVEMBER 16

"A banker is a fellow who lends you his umbrella when the sun is shining, but wants it back the minute it begins to rain."

—MARK TWAIN

20 ___ _____

_____

_____

_____

20 ___ _____

_____

_____

_____

20 ___ _____

_____

_____

_____

20 ___ _____

_____

_____

_____

20 ___ _____

_____

_____

_____

NOVEMBER 17

"I bet a funny thing about driving a car off a cliff is, while you're in midair, you still hit those brakes."

—JACK HANDEY

20 ___ _____

_____

_____

_____

20 ___ _____

_____

_____

_____

20 ___ _____

_____

_____

_____

20 ___ _____

_____

_____

_____

20 ___ _____

_____

_____

_____

NOVEMBER 18

"Few of us ever live in the present. We are forever anticipating what is to come or remembering what has gone."

—LOUIS L'AMOUR

20 ___ _____

_____

_____

_____

20 ___ _____

_____

_____

_____

20 ___ _____

_____

_____

_____

20 ___ _____

_____

_____

_____

20 ___ _____

_____

_____

_____

NOVEMBER 19

"Never underestimate the stimulation of eccentricity."

—Neil Simon

20 ___ _____

_____

_____

_____

_____

20 ___ _____

_____

_____

_____

_____

20 ___ _____

_____

_____

_____

_____

20 ___ _____

_____

_____

_____

_____

20 ___ _____

_____

_____

_____

_____

NOVEMBER 20

"Women are made to be loved, not understood."

—OSCAR WILDE

20 ___ _____

_____

_____

_____

_____

20 ___ _____

_____

_____

_____

_____

20 ___ _____

_____

_____

_____

_____

20 ___ _____

_____

_____

_____

_____

20 ___ _____

_____

_____

_____

_____

NOVEMBER 21

"Famous remarks are very seldom quoted correctly."

—SIMEON STRUNSKY

20 ___ _____

_____

_____

_____

_____

20 ___ _____

_____

_____

_____

_____

20 ___ _____

_____

_____

_____

_____

20 ___ _____

_____

_____

_____

_____

20 ___ _____

_____

_____

_____

_____

NOVEMBER 22

"Bureaucracy defends the status quo long past the time when the quo has lost its status."

20 ___ _____

_____

_____

_____

_____

20 ___ _____

_____

_____

_____

_____

20 ___ _____

_____

_____

_____

_____

20 ___ _____

_____

_____

_____

_____

20 ___ _____

_____

_____

_____

_____

NOVEMBER 23

"The ability to quote is a serviceable substitute for wit."

—MAUGHAM

20 ___ _____

_____

_____

_____

_____

20 ___ _____

_____

_____

_____

_____

20 ___ _____

_____

_____

_____

_____

20 ___ _____

_____

_____

_____

_____

20 ___ _____

_____

_____

_____

_____

NOVEMBER 24

"I think I've discovered the secret of life - you just hang around until you get used to it."

—Charles M. Schulz

20 ___ _____

_____

_____

_____

_____

20 ___ _____

_____

_____

_____

_____

20 ___ _____

_____

_____

_____

_____

20 ___ _____

_____

_____

_____

_____

20 ___ _____

_____

_____

_____

_____

NOVEMBER 25

"Great things are not accomplished by those who yield to trends and fads and popular opinion."

—JACK KEROUAC

20 ___ _____

_____

_____

_____

_____

20 ___ _____

_____

_____

_____

_____

20 ___ _____

_____

_____

_____

_____

20 ___ _____

_____

_____

_____

_____

20 ___ _____

_____

_____

_____

_____

NOVEMBER 26

"If you were me, then I'd be you, and if I were you, then I'd hide somewhere far away."

20 ___ _____

_____

_____

_____

_____

20 ___ _____

_____

_____

_____

_____

20 ___ _____

_____

_____

_____

_____

20 ___ _____

_____

_____

_____

_____

20 ___ _____

_____

_____

_____

_____

NOVEMBER 27

"Everyone seems to have a clear idea of how other people should lead their lives, but none about his or her own."

—PAULO COLEHO

20 ___ _____

_____

_____

_____

_____

20 ___ _____

_____

_____

_____

_____

20 ___ _____

_____

_____

_____

_____

20 ___ _____

_____

_____

_____

_____

20 ___ _____

_____

_____

_____

_____

NOVEMBER 28

"A creative man is motivated by the desire to achieve, not by the desire to beat others."

—AYN RAND

20 __ _____

_____

_____

_____

_____

20 __ _____

_____

_____

_____

_____

20 __ _____

_____

_____

_____

_____

20 __ _____

_____

_____

_____

_____

20 __ _____

_____

_____

_____

_____

NOVEMBER 29

"The most exciting phrase to hear in science, the one that heralds the most discoveries, is not 'Eureka!' but 'That's funny...'"

—ISAAC ASIMOV

20 ___ _____

_____

_____

_____

20 ___ _____

_____

_____

_____

20 ___ _____

_____

_____

_____

20 ___ _____

_____

_____

_____

20 ___ _____

_____

_____

_____

NOVEMBER 30

"Writing is a way of talking without being interrupted."

—JULES RENARD

20 ___ _____

_____

_____

_____

_____

20 ___ _____

_____

_____

_____

_____

20 ___ _____

_____

_____

_____

_____

20 ___ _____

_____

_____

_____

_____

20 ___ _____

_____

_____

_____

_____

DECEMBER 1

"If the self-help books worked, it would be a shrinking industry, not a growing one."

—STEVE MARABOLI

20 ___ _____

_____

_____

_____

20 ___ _____

_____

_____

_____

20 ___ _____

_____

_____

_____

20 ___ _____

_____

_____

_____

20 ___ _____

_____

_____

_____

DECEMBER 2

"To love oneself is the beginning of a lifelong romance."

—OSCAR WILDE

20 ___ _____

_____

_____

_____

20 ___ _____

_____

_____

_____

20 ___ _____

_____

_____

_____

20 ___ _____

_____

_____

_____

20 ___ _____

_____

_____

_____

DECEMBER 3

"You should eat a waffle! You can't be sad if you eat a waffle!"

—LAUREN MYRACLE

20 ___

20 ___

20 ___

20 ___

20 ___

DECEMBER 4

"Sometimes the road less traveled is less traveled for a reason."

—JERRY SEINFELD

20 ___

_____

20 ___

_____

20 ___

_____

20 ___

_____

20 ___

_____

DECEMBER 5

"Real stupidity beats artificial intelligence every time."

—TERRY PRATCHETT

20 ___ _____

_____

_____

_____

20 ___ _____

_____

_____

_____

20 ___ _____

_____

_____

_____

20 ___ _____

_____

_____

_____

20 ___ _____

_____

_____

_____

DECEMBER 6

"Confidence is ignorance. If you're feeling cocky, it's because there's something you don't know."

—EOIN COLFER

20 ___ _____

_____

_____

_____

_____

20 ___ _____

_____

_____

_____

_____

20 ___ _____

_____

_____

_____

_____

20 ___ _____

_____

_____

_____

_____

20 ___ _____

_____

_____

_____

_____

DECEMBER 7

"If you're going to kick authority in the teeth, you might as well use two feet."

—KEITH RICHARDS

20 ___ _____

_____

_____

_____

20 ___ _____

_____

_____

_____

20 ___ _____

_____

_____

_____

20 ___ _____

_____

_____

_____

20 ___ _____

_____

_____

_____

DECEMBER 8

"All the secrets of the world are contained in books. Read at your own risk."

—LEMONY SNICKET

20 ___ _____

_____

_____

_____

_____

20 ___ _____

_____

_____

_____

_____

20 ___ _____

_____

_____

_____

_____

20 ___ _____

_____

_____

_____

_____

20 ___ _____

_____

_____

_____

_____

DECEMBER 9

"Either write something worth reading or do something worth writing."

—BENJAMIN FRANKLIN

20 16 Today I am discouraged. Discouraged that my discipline is not as it should. Just see how long it has been since my last entry! My goal is to be as effective as possible as a follower of Christ, as a husband, as a father, and as a pastor. Discipline is the path.

20 ___

20 ___

20 ___

20 ___

DECEMBER 10

"Harry was left to ponder in silence the depths to which girls would sink to get revenge."

—J.K. ROWLING

20 ___ _____

_____

_____

_____

20 ___ _____

_____

_____

_____

20 ___ _____

_____

_____

_____

20 ___ _____

_____

_____

_____

20 ___ _____

_____

_____

_____

DECEMBER 11

"Life isn't finding shelter in the storm.
It's about learning to dance in the rain."

—SHERRILYN KENYON

20 ___ _____

_____

_____

_____

20 ___ _____

_____

_____

_____

20 ___ _____

_____

_____

_____

20 ___ _____

_____

_____

_____

20 ___ _____

_____

_____

_____

DECEMBER 12

"Maybe this world is another planet's hell."

—ALDOUS HUXLEY

20 16 Chan turned 18 yesterday. Unreal. Despite healthy & growing numbers @ the church (over 400) for second week, I'm feeling discontent. It's like I should know what to do next. One thing I do know, today needs to be day one of gym.

20 __

20 __

20 __

20 __

DECEMBER 13

"Too bad that all the people who know how to run the country are busy driving taxicabs and cutting hair."

—GEORGE BURNS

20 ___ _____

_____

_____

_____

20 ___ _____

_____

_____

_____

20 ___ _____

_____

_____

_____

20 ___ _____

_____

_____

_____

20 ___ _____

_____

_____

_____

DECEMBER 14

"You can safely assume you've created God in your own image when it turns out that God hates all the same people you do."

—ANNE LAMOTT

20 ___ _____

_____

_____

_____

20 ___ _____

_____

_____

_____

20 ___ _____

_____

_____

_____

20 ___ _____

_____

_____

_____

20 ___ _____

_____

_____

_____

DECEMBER 15

"Indeed I have always been of the opinion that hard work is simply the refuge of people who have nothing to do."

—OSCAR WILDE

20 ___ _____
_____
_____
_____

20 ___ _____
_____
_____
_____

20 ___ _____
_____
_____
_____

20 ___ _____
_____
_____
_____

20 ___ _____
_____
_____
_____

DECEMBER 16

"Any sufficiently advanced technology is indistinguishable from magic."

—ARTHUR C. CLARKE

20 ___ _____

_____

_____

_____

20 ___ _____

_____

_____

_____

20 ___ _____

_____

_____

_____

20 ___ _____

_____

_____

_____

20 ___ _____

_____

_____

_____

DECEMBER 17

"Sometimes I wonder whether the world is being run by smart people who are putting us on or by imbeciles who really mean it."

—MARK TWAIN

20 ___ _____

_____

_____

_____

_____

20 ___ _____

_____

_____

_____

_____

20 ___ _____

_____

_____

_____

_____

20 ___ _____

_____

_____

_____

_____

20 ___ _____

_____

_____

_____

_____

DECEMBER 18

"Nothing ever fatigues me, but doing what I do not like."

—JANE AUSTEN

20 ___ _____

_____

_____

_____

_____

20 ___ _____

_____

_____

_____

_____

20 ___ _____

_____

_____

_____

_____

20 ___ _____

_____

_____

_____

_____

20 ___ _____

_____

_____

_____

_____

DECEMBER 19

"We spend our lives making livings."

—Jonathan Safran Foer

20 ___ _____

_____

_____

_____

_____

20 ___ _____

_____

_____

_____

_____

20 ___ _____

_____

_____

_____

_____

20 ___ _____

_____

_____

_____

_____

20 ___ _____

_____

_____

_____

_____

DECEMBER 20

"I generally avoid temptation unless I can't resist it."

—MAE WEST

20 ___ _____

_____

_____

_____

20 ___ _____

_____

_____

_____

20 ___ _____

_____

_____

_____

20 ___ _____

_____

_____

_____

20 ___ _____

_____

_____

_____

DECEMBER 21

"Television--a medium. So called because it is neither rare nor well done."

—ERNIE KOVACS

20 ___ _____

_____

_____

_____

_____

20 ___ _____

_____

_____

_____

_____

20 ___ _____

_____

_____

_____

_____

20 ___ _____

_____

_____

_____

_____

20 ___ _____

_____

_____

_____

_____

DECEMBER 22

"Today is the sort of day where the sun only comes up to humiliate you."

—CHUCK PALAHNIUK

20 __ _____

_____

_____

_____

20 __ _____

_____

_____

_____

20 __ _____

_____

_____

_____

20 __ _____

_____

_____

_____

20 __ _____

_____

_____

_____

DECEMBER 23

"I stopped believing in Santa Claus when I was six. Mother took me to see him in a department store and he asked for my autograph."

—SHIRLEY TEMPLE

20 ___ _____

_____

_____

_____

20 ___ _____

_____

_____

_____

20 ___ _____

_____

_____

_____

20 ___ _____

_____

_____

_____

20 ___ _____

_____

_____

_____

DECEMBER 24

"You can tell a lot about a person by the way (s)he handles three things: a rainy day, lost luggage, and tangled Christmas tree lights."
—MAYA ANGELOU

20 ___ _____

_____

_____

_____

20 ___ _____

_____

_____

_____

20 ___ _____

_____

_____

_____

20 ___ _____

_____

_____

_____

20 ___ _____

_____

_____

_____

DECEMBER 25

"Blessed is the season which engages the whole world in a conspiracy of love."

—HAMILTON WRIGHT MABIE

20 __ _____

_____

_____

_____

_____

20 __ _____

_____

_____

_____

_____

20 __ _____

_____

_____

_____

_____

20 __ _____

_____

_____

_____

_____

20 __ _____

_____

_____

_____

_____

DECEMBER 26

"Don't cry because it's over, smile because it happened."

—DR. SEUSS

20 ___ _____

_____

_____

_____

20 ___ _____

_____

_____

_____

20 ___ _____

_____

_____

_____

20 ___ _____

_____

_____

_____

20 ___ _____

_____

_____

_____

DECEMBER 27

"This must be Thursday. I never could get the hang of Thursdays."

—Douglas Adams

20 ___ _____

_____

_____

_____

20 ___ _____

_____

_____

_____

20 ___ _____

_____

_____

_____

20 ___ _____

_____

_____

_____

20 ___ _____

_____

_____

_____

DECEMBER 28

"The shortest distance between two points is always under construction."

—REBECCA MCCLANAHAN

20 ___ _____

_____

_____

_____

20 ___ _____

_____

_____

_____

20 ___ _____

_____

_____

_____

20 ___ _____

_____

_____

_____

20 ___ _____

_____

_____

_____

DECEMBER 29

"Life is not measured by the number of breaths we take, but by the moments that take our breath away."

—MAYA ANGELOU

20 ___ _____

_____

_____

_____

20 ___ _____

_____

_____

_____

20 ___ _____

_____

_____

_____

20 ___ _____

_____

_____

_____

20 ___ _____

_____

_____

_____

DECEMBER 30

"Dance like no one is watching. Sing like no one is listening. Love like you've never been hurt and live like it's heaven on Earth."

—MARK TWAIN

20 __ _____

_____

_____

_____

_____

20 __ _____

_____

_____

_____

_____

20 __ _____

_____

_____

_____

_____

20 __ _____

_____

_____

_____

_____

20 __ _____

_____

_____

_____

_____

DECEMBER 31

*"Be who you are and say what you feel, because those who mind
don't matter, and those who matter don't mind."*

—DR. SEUSS

20 __ _____

_____

_____

_____

20 __ _____

_____

_____

_____

20 __ _____

_____

_____

_____

20 __ _____

_____

_____

_____

20 __ _____

_____

_____

_____

IMPORTANT DATES

IMPORTANT DATES

YEAR 1 GOALS

_____

_____

_____

_____

_____

_____

_____

_____

_____

_____

_____

_____

_____

_____

_____

_____

_____

_____

_____

_____

_____

_____

_____

YEAR 2 GOALS

YEAR 3 GOALS

YEAR 4 GOALS

YEAR 5 GOALS

www.WickedSassy.com

55945000R00212

Made in the USA
Lexington, KY
07 October 2016